CRITICAL ACCLAIM
for Martha Friedman's
LIFE-CHANGING BOOK

OVERCOMING THE
FEAR OF SUCCESS

OVERCÖMING THE FEAR OF SUCCESS

MARTHA FRIEDMAN, Ph. D.

WARNER BOOKS

A Warner Communications Company

For Chick
who helped me all along the way

In this world there are only two tragedies. One is not getting what one wants and the other is getting it.

—Oscar Wilde

Contents

Contents /

Preface

T<small>HIS BOOK</small> will not solve all of your problems. But if you have a fear of success—and you'll learn if you do or not in these pages—my hope is that you'll find enough material here to set you on the road to recognizing and overcoming your fear.

Most psychological problems are complicated and sometimes elusive. If I were writing a professional paper on the fear of success, I would have to qualify statements so often that those of you who do have this fear could end up even more confused than you are now. Therefore in these pages you'll find plain, untechnical language and as few qualifiers as possible.

You'll see that my orientation is strictly psychological. I'll not be dealing with biochemical or genetic influences on human behavior. Psychic/social influences are what interest me and where my training has been.

These pages contain case histories of people who

have or have had a fear of success. All names of students, patients, friends, acquaintances, relatives have been changed. At times I have combined histories when I thought that the underlying dynamics and the real life manifestation of the problems were similar.

I have used the generic "his" throughout these pages which, of course, includes "her." At the moment, unfortunately, there is no grammatically smooth way around this problem.

I wish to thank Dr. Irving Bieber for the expansion of my understanding of the theory of the fear of success. Paul Himmel, and Esther Benson for their help and encouragement with this book. To Dolores Klaich goes my gratitude for listening to my voice and assisting me in the preparation of this material. To Helene Shapiro goes my appreciation for her funding of my New School lecture series. And special thanks to Ruth Van Doran, Director of Human Relations, The New School. And, lastly, I am indebted to the many students and patients who helped me in the data collection for this book.

MARTHA FRIEDMAN

Our Psyches Are Not of One Mind

NOT TOO LONG AGO in New York City, where I live, I flagged a taxi and asked the cabbie to take me to Eleventh Street between Fifth and Sixth Avenues. When we neared Fourteenth Street, the driver asked me where exactly I was going.

"To the New School," I told him.

"Why you going there?"

"I'm teaching a class."

"What're you teaching?"

"Overcoming the Fear of Success."

"You mean to say you got people there so successful they're worried about it? Boy, what some people do to make a living."

Nobody ever believes taxi driver stories; people think writers make them up to make a point. Well, this is a true story and my point is that this cabbie's reaction to the mention of the psychological problem called the fear of success is typical of the pervasive skepticism I've encountered since I first started observing the phenomenon more than two decades ago.

On first hearing, very few people seem to get it. *Fear* of success? What's she talking about? It doesn't make sense. Nobody in his right mind is afraid of success. On the contrary. Everyone wants success—and badly. That's what it's all about.

Isn't it?

"Don't listen to her," a well-known songwriter told a group of my students. "There's no such thing as the fear of success. My worst song won an Academy Award. I love being a success. . . ."

On and on he went one night when he visited my class until a student raised her hand and asked him:

"Did you always want to be a songwriter?"

"No," he said. "I wanted to be a pianist."

Student: "Why didn't you become a pianist?"

Songwriter: "My parents were poor. Since I was sixteen I wrote songs and they made money. I helped out with the family."

Student: "But you became rich and famous; why didn't you switch when you had made more than enough money?"

Songwriter: "Well, for some unknown reason, I kept burning my fingers."

Student: "Oh."

". . . for some unknown reason." It calls to mind stories I have heard of people who become mysteriously overweight or inexplicably pregnant—

splendid examples of self-sabotage, along with burnt fingers (if you're a pianist), of the fear of success.

A few weeks after the songwriter addressed my class, I ran into him at a wedding. He kept circling me and pointing at me; it was like a comedy routine:

"Don't listen to her! There's no such thing as the fear of success! That woman's crazy!"

Why such resistance?

I well may be mildly crazed at certain rare moments in certain aspects of my life—aren't we all at one time or another?—but on the subject at hand I'm here, in all sanity, to tell you that there is such a thing as the fear of success and that:

• it is a significant problem in our society
• it resides mostly in the realm of the unconscious
• it stems from early childhood experiences
• it is reinforced by cultural and family double messages
• it manifests itself in self-sabotaging behavior that leads to unsatisfactory work lives and/or love lives
• it can be overcome, or at least modified

By success I don't mean, quick, who can make the most money the fastest? For advice on this sort of success—style over substance—see any number of current success self-help books and articles; they are full of superficial guidance for superficial glory, pseudo help for pseudo strength.

This does not mean that I am against money. In our society, people get rewarded for being rich. It's nice to get rewarded. It's nice to be rich. A little tinsel and glitter never hurt anybody. However, money in itself, as everyone keeps telling us but we seldom believe, does not mean success as I'll define it. And outrageous amounts of money in a land of unequal opportunity are obscene.

The sort of success I'm talking about is not defined in terms of fortune and fame and power and prestige and possessions (although it may include these externals, all icing on the cake). I am talking about *internal success*, the lack of which makes external success, although perhaps fleetingly fulfilling, certainly in the final analysis painfully hollow. It's not without reason that the phrase, "Is that all there is?" has become a refrain for many of us.

The sort of success I mean consists of this: getting to do what you really want to do in your work life and in your love life, doing it very well, and feeling good about yourself doing it. The fear of success is *not* getting what you really want because you unconsciously feel you don't deserve it.

In our culture, success is usually measured in terms of work achievement; thus most of these pages will deal with our professional lives. We will also consider the fear of success as it manifests itself in our emotional lives, our love lives. Freud's premise is that a healthy individual is one who can love and one who can work. These are our two major functions in life, and to be successful at both is not all that common an occurrence; if we are successful at all, we are much more likely to be very successful at one and less successful at the other. More on this trade-off shortly.

I should point out here that I am concerned with

overcoming the fear of success only as it pertains to these United States, to our success-obsessed culture. I am not talking about the fear of success in Cambodia, or even in Japan, where a tradition of the nobility of failure (remember the kamikaze missions, for example) exists within a boomingly successful economy—thus giving the Japanese their own particular set of psychological problems.

I am also not dealing with tragic reality factors in our society that may preclude success. Violence, serious illness, war, oppression, racism, poverty—any may bring tragedy to the human experience. A few years ago when I served on a task force to investigate sexism in a public school system, I learned about a vocational class for mentally retarded children in which the boys were being trained to be hospital lab technicians and the girls to be servants. This, obviously, has nothing to do with the psychologically induced malady called the fear of success but, rather, with deeply ingrained societal sexism *and* bad vocational guidance.

Not everyone can have success. There are human tragedies. We still do live, even with all the progress we've made, in a land of unequal opportunity. But for those of us who do stand a chance, or even half a chance, the question becomes: Why do we so often self-destructively arrange our own unequal opportunities?

We don't *not* reach our goals because of bad luck, or because of not being in the right place at the right time, or because of not getting the right break. Some of these may figure in the denial of external success, but they have nothing to do with internal success, with the ways in which we ourselves—outside forces beside the point—sabotage our self-fulfillment. All those sinister outside forces that are conspiring against our happiness will not concern us here. It is our self-inflicted catastrophes at which we'll take a look.

The fear of success seems a paradox. On a conscious level, no one is afraid of success; everyone wants to be successful. But on an unconscious level, in that place few of us ever really explore, it's often quite a different story. There, in the unconscious, is where many of us do our best, without realizing it, to ensure that success is never reached or, if it is, that it doesn't last.

For many of us, to admit that unknown machinations in our psyches can bring about self-defeating behavior can mean we aren't really in control of our lives after all. What could lead to greater resistance? Especially these days when even with our conscious behavior we can control so little of our environment. No wonder so many of us refuse to deal with our unconscious. Who has time for such delving? Most of us are too busy striving for success.

A few years ago, a young student who had taken my course in Overcoming the Fear of Success for credit handed in a paper to make up an incomplete. In the paper he related a poor academic and work history. He said he wanted to be a social worker so he could help people. Later in the paper he reiterated this wish: "I want to complete your course to bring me one step closer to that goal of helping trouble people." (!) He titled the paper "Fear of Overcoming Success."

Don't tell me that this young man's unconscious was not at work.

It's almost impossible for me to believe that there

are as many people as there are who refuse to acknowledge—slips of the tongue notwithstanding—the importance of the unconscious in determining behavior.
Maybe even you have some trouble with this? Some
discomfort? Discomfort or not, in order to come along
with me through these pages, you'll have to acknowledge
certain elementary psychological principles. The first
is that you'll have to grant the existence of the unconscious and you'll have to accept the enormity of the
influence it exerts on our behavior.

The seed for the theory of the fear of success can be
found in a principle first formulated by Freud; that is,
when we finally get what we really want, it all falls apart
for us. He wrote:

> . . . people occasionally fall ill precisely because a deeply
> rooted and long cherished wish has come to fulfillment.
> It seems then as though they could not endure their
> bliss, for of the causative connection between this ful-
> fillment and the falling ill there can be no question.*

By "falling ill," Freud meant engaging in self-defeating behavior, both psychological and physiological. Depression, phobias, masochism, and addiction to drugs
are psychological disorders that have been readily laid at
the door of the psyche. It took longer to recognize that
physiological problems such as migraine headaches,
ulcers, arthritis, and colitis may have stress and tension
at their root. Or, as comic Mel Brooks facetiously de-
scribes this phenomenon, "People let their hearts attack them."

* Sigmund Freud, "Those Wrecked by Success" (1915), in *Collected
Papers*, Vol. IV (London: Hogarth, 1949), p. 324.

In addition to Freud's basic theory of falling apart *after* a goal is reached, you can have a fear of success if you fall apart *just as* the goal is being reached, and you can have a fear of success if you never even get to first base with the goal.

At this point, I should tell you that I am not a strict Freudian in my therapeutic orientation, even though I sometimes feel I have a pipeline to Freud since I was analyzed by a woman who was analyzed by Marie Bonaparte who was analyzed by Freud. In the present controversy over his work, I would like to say that just because Freud said it doesn't make it wrong.

In addition to dealing with your unconscious, you must also be prepared to recognize a basic contradiction in our culture. Although my emphasis in this book is on the intrapsychic dynamics that lead to the fear of success, there are also cultural forces that contribute to the problem. The basic contradiction is: our culture comes through loud and clear on how important it is to win, to be a success, but at the same time, and paradoxically, it tells us to lose. It's all right, somehow even virtuous, to lose:

- one man's gain, another man's sorrow
- the meek shall inherit the earth
- it's not whether you win or lose that counts, but how you play the game
- all good things must come to an end

On the other hand, there are the words of that great American thinker, football coach Vince Lombardi:

"Winning is not the main thing, it's the only thing."

The tug of war that results from such cultural adages

is enough to make me wonder why we aren't all, each and every one of us, stark raving mad. Damned if we win; damned if we lose. An awful double bind. Conflict. Guilt. Anxiety. Paralysis.

Additionally, our culture bombards us almost daily with examples of that peculiarly American institution, the overnight instant success. There are hundreds of modern Horatio Alger stories, hundreds of role models. Just pull yourself up by your bootstraps, kid . . . only in America. You too can be . . . Elvis Presley! Janis Joplin! Freddie Prinze! Richard Milhous Nixon!

While we climb for our particular piece of the American dream, we fail to take in the significance of the lives of these once "successful" people. Why, when they had "everything," did they self-destruct? Through an understanding of the dynamics of the fear of success, I believe you'll be able to see why a rock star at the height of his career could commit suicide or die a drug-oblivious death; why a Hollywood legend of the past could end up on the back ward of a state mental hospital; why a Richard Milhous Nixon, when all was said and done, did not destroy those White House tapes, thus effectively choreographing his own destruction.

We fail to take in these disturbing elements of our competitive American way of life because we're too busy trying to be successful. No one has warned us that success may be hazardous to our mental health. By the time we do digest some public figure's death or destruction, our culture has already spewed forth another instant success to take his place. Just turn to your latest issue of *People* magazine.

Not all of us, but a significant number of us have a

fear of success. And I'm not just talking about rock stars and Presidents. The phenomenon exists in all walks of life. It doesn't matter what sex you are, what age, what you do for a living, what social class you are a part of, how much education you've had, what your sexual orientation is, what interests you have. If certain factors have been operating in your psyche, factors that were incorporated in early childhood, you may very well be living with a fear of success—even though to you the thought may appear to be completely aberrant.

Even understanding this much, it still sounds ludicrous to say that trying to get what we want, especially if our wants are realistic, may place us in jeopardy. Why is it so difficult to get what we want and to feel entitled to it once we get it? Many of our goals are realistic, our dreams achievable, our fantasies within reach. Few of us are grandiose.

As we will see, the answer to this question will be different for each of us, for we are talking about unconscious self-defeating behavior, things going on in our psyches that may be keeping us from success—and Lord knows our psyches are not of one mind.

2 /

I Just Can't Get It All Together

To *get* WHAT WE WANT, we first have to *know* what we want, and for that we have to know who we really are.

It's too bad that these last words, "who we really are," have become a sort of joke, buzzwords to put down the Me phenomenon that we are in the process of experiencing. It's a shame, because the basic concept of Know Thyself is absolutely essential to overcoming the fear of success. Too many of us have faulty perceptions of ourselves; we'll get nowhere until we come up with honest appraisals. Therefore Know Thyself as a concept, no matter how damaged by certain aspects of the human potential movement, is valid.

Any number of self-help success books advocate just this. But then what? Most promise that with self-awareness and self-knowledge, all things are possible.

Wrong. What usually happens to people who have a fear of success is that they do a lot of soul-searching and then say, "All right, I know myself—I'm a mess." Obviously what needs getting at is *why* we feel a mess, *why* we have such low self-esteem, how did feelings of inadequacy, emptiness, unworthiness, fraudulence develop. And for the answers to these questions, no formula how-to success book will help.

These books say things like: "Are you feeling depressed about losing a job? A lover?" Then they advise, "Go to a party; put on a happy face; who knows who you might meet there." Or they say, "Feeling guilty is a waste of time." Both of these pieces of advice are just so much hogwash. Neither deals with the root of such depression or guilt. In fact, such advice easily produces a still greater sense of unhappiness about nonachievement. Simplistic how-to books don't deal with the underlying dynamics in our individual psyches that make us lead less-than-fulfilling lives. All one really gets from reading them is a Band-Aid over a cancer.

Nor do such books deal with those internalized negative messages—parental and societal—that keep us from our full potential. Certainly this was the case with the rash of how-to sex manuals that bombarded us in the late 1960s and the 1970s telling us how to be successful sex partners.

If such books could do the trick, then the widely read *The Joy of Sex*, a very good book in its way, would have liberated all of sexual America. However, our inhibitions about sex are not dispensed with so readily. In spite of the so-called sexual revolution, we're still pleasure-inhibited about sex. *The Joy of Sex* did positively reassure people that what they were thinking, feeling, and doing in bed was not deviant. However, it did little for those burdened with layers and layers of internalized messages (both parental and societal), messages that said that sex in general is dirty, perverse, sinful, bad—except when used for procreation in a marriage bed.

Message from mother to daughter: "You can replace money, darling, but not virginity. However, I want you to know that sex is beautiful."

Message from father to son: "One small slip, son, and you're stuck for life. However, sex is healthy. Just make sure you wash after—and not with Ivory soap. Fels Naphtha always worked for me."

It is said that in matters sexual we function at less than 50 percent of our potential. With messages such as those above, I'm surprised the percentage isn't lower.

Because we must discover the underlying psychological reasons as to why we sabotage ourselves in our sex lives and elsewhere and, as mentioned, our psyches are not of one mind, there is no single formula to follow to overcome the fear of success. We are just too complex as individuals, and have spent too much of our time becoming so, for any one formula to work. We have to take into consideration the differences, the uniqueness, and the very important time sequence of experience that make up the totality of a person. There are no shortcuts to self-integration.

One of the best ways to start on an exploration to see whether or not you have a fear of success is to read the following list of success-inhibiting characteris-

tics. Can you relate to any—not all but any—of the
following fear-of-success symptoms?

Do you feel that if people really knew you they wouldn't
    like you?

Do you fear exposure of something about yourself?

Do you feel deep down that you are a fraud?

Do you think you are always pulling the wool over
    people's eyes?

Is feeling good a strange state for you?

Does feeling bad feel good to you?

Do you feel that good feelings can't last?

Do you feel you are appreciated for your hard luck
    stories?

Do you dilute good times with reflections of past sad-
    ness or future catastrophes?

Do you refer to yourself as a casualty of bad luck?

Do you prefer the sidelines to center stage?

Are you reluctant to play a leading role?

When you get something you want, do you find you
    don't want it anymore?

When you reach a goal that you have been striving for,
    do you feel, "Is that all there is?"

Is it easier to spend money on others than on yourself?

Do you feel competition is the root of all evil?

Do you feel you are the root of all evil when competing?

Do you feel you are better than the work you are doing?

Is your job boring?

Do you have a pattern of switching jobs frequently?

Are you afraid to leave a long-term job for a better offer?

Are you a jack-of-all-trades and master of none?

Are you a workaholic?

Can you not get a job?

Can you not get a job that you like?

Can you not hold a job?

Can you not advance on the job?

Do you hate or even dislike your job?

Are you always late no matter how hard you try to be on time?

Do you have difficulty making decisions?

Do you feel there are too many alternatives in life to commit yourself to any one thing?

Can you accomplish something only if there is a deadline?

Are you a perfectionist?

Do you fear making a mistake?

Would you rather be well liked than competent?

Do you procrastinate?

Do you kill time?

Does free time make you anxious?

Do Sundays depress you?

Does it sometimes feel to you as if you have been engaged in a lifetime pursuit of defeat?

Do you feel you are a success at home and a failure at work?

Do you feel you are a success at work and a failure at home?

Are you the family pessimist, always predicting gloom and doom?

Were you the preferred child in the family, Papa's little darling or Mama's little man?

Were you the scapegoat in your family?

Were you the rotten apple in the barrel?

Were you the rock of Gibraltar?

Are you generous to a fault, mostly wanting to be liked no matter what the cost?

Are you aggressive to a fault, mostly trying to best people no matter how you alienate them?

Are you detached to a fault, fearing intimacy or closeness?

Are you repelled by people who are attracted to you?

Are you attracted to people who are repelled by you?

Are you attracted only to people who are unavailable to you?

Do you have short-term relationships that end disastrously?

Do you avoid relationships to eliminate the possibility of rejection?

Do you believe that everyone in the world is coupled except the creeps?

When something goes wrong, do you feel somehow responsible, even if you know you're not?

Do you fake orgasms?

Do you ejaculate prematurely?

Do you use sex as a weapon?

Are you too shy to tell your partner what feels good to you?

Are you shy?

Do you feel sex is too strenuous if you have to get up early in the morning?

Do you feel that sex is boring?

Do you feel too fat for sex?

Is losing weight a losing battle for you?

Do you repeat mistakes?

Are you a perpetual student?

Are you satisfied with the middle range in school?

Do you usually cram instead of studying?

Do you frequently change your area of study?

Are you a high school dropout?

Are you a Ph.D. dropout?

Do you spend more money than you earn?

Do you live by credit cards alone?

Do you always pick up the tab?

Are you a miser who predicts ending up in a poverty pocket?

Can you accept praise openly and directly?

Or do you downgrade compliments?

> "You're looking good."
> "Except for these ten extra pounds."
> "Great performance."
> "Nah, I was off in Act II."
> "Delicious dinner."
> "The roast was overdone."

Have you ever said, "I just can't get it all together and I don't know why"?

Do you have an overall feeling that things could be better for you?

Are you afraid to move, even to a better neighborhood?

Do you believe "It's lonely at the top"?

Do you miss the hungry years?

Do you feel it's all over?

If you related to any of these questions, chances are you have a fear of success. The umbrella question under which all the others rest is: Do you feel you lead a rewarding life? In other words, are you happy in your work and with your emotional partner? Even those of us who are relatively happy could be happier. The great majority of us function way below our capacity. We sabotage ourselves in little ways all the time. There are degrees of the fear of success. It ranges from being a mild neurosis to being a paralyzing phobia.

It is common when one first starts to understand the theory of the fear of success to see it in full flower— in others. Did your mother thrive on telling hard luck stories? Did your father live only for his work? Is your spouse or lover detached, unable to handle intimacy? This is a first step. Then, with serious motivation, we can try to break through our own defenses to face our own past and present destructive patterns. Why is it, for example, that you have a pattern of getting into relationships that end disastrously? Why is it, for example, that you always feel better than the work you're doing?

Habit has a compulsive hold on us. It's the compulsive nature of self-defeating behavior that makes simplistic how-to success strategies worse than useless.

Some people who cannot understand what is meant by the fear of success say, "Oh, she means the fear of failure." No, I do not.

I first began to suspect the existence of a psychological problem called the fear of success (rather than the fear of failure) twenty-five years ago when I encountered groups of very bright children who could not read.

I was hired as a consultant by a wealthy suburban school system that was filled with what are known as "advantaged" children. My job was to concentrate on those students who, although bright, could not learn to read. The boys (a reading disability has been primarily a boy's problem; if a girl had it, she was said to be male-identified or dyslexic) came from upper-middle-class achievement-oriented families. High academic marks, as one boy told me, were required, not just encouraged. Any grade less than an A was frowned upon. Some of the parents were grooming their offspring for Harvard and Yale and thought that the ability of six-year-olds to read second-grade readers was only average reading ability for getting ahead. The boys who couldn't read at all were certainly in bad trouble.

The pressure on these children was enormous. Some who were severely blocked in their ability to read had parents who focused everything on external success. Thus learning to read had little to do with enjoying life and literature, a form of internal success, but everything to do with getting ahead in life, for the most part monetarily.

Generally, a reading disability in a child is an indicator that something is amiss, either an emotional disturbance, a neurological or perceptual difficulty, immaturity, poor teaching, or any combination thereof. After I had weeded out some of the then more recognizable causes for the boys' inability to read, I was left with the problems of some boys for which there seemed to be no discernible causes. These were the days, the early 1950s, before the importance of the influence of family interaction on the psyche of a child was fully realized.

The study of family dynamics is a relatively new field, only about thirty years old. Before the turn of the century, when a child became disturbed, either slightly or very, the trouble was usually attributed to demons. Later it was decided it was all Máma's fault; she was the demon. However, mental health professionals saw that they were sending home too many stabilized schizophrenic children-patients only to have them revert to their schizophrenia the moment they stepped through their family front door—whether there was a Mama in residence or not. It became important to look closely at the child's family dynamics. Today, with the revelatory work of pioneers such as Dr. Nathan Ackerman, we are acknowledging the importance of the influence of the entire family constellation on a child's psyche. This is not to say that a child's genetic composition is discounted. Some of us are born more vulnerable than others.

In understanding the fear of success, none of my training has been as important as that of the study of family life. To understand the competition patterns in families and to see how we are programmed for winning or losing is to understand how a fear of success can develop.

After working for a while with the remainder of the boys who could not learn to read, it became obvious that they had some sort of an investment in not learning. Odd as it seemed, they were afraid to succeed. Something was going on in their families that in their minds caused a highly negative reading disability to serve a positive purpose.

In many cases, that purpose was to shore up their parents' shaky marriage, to keep their parents together. The scenario goes like this: Johnny's parents are fighting. Johnny feels the security of his home life is threatened. There is a phone call from Johnny's teacher who says, "Your son is having trouble learning to read." Johnny's parents stop fighting and focus their attention on their underachieving son.

As long as Johnny has his reading problem, as long as he keeps failing, he feels that his parents will refrain from fighting and they will not split up (abandon Johnny). As we will see, children will go to incredible lengths, even fail, to keep their families intact; the fear of abandonment is just too frightening. How many times have you heard, "They stayed together for the children." We seldom think about the children who fell apart to keep their parents together.

These "advantaged" boys were not afraid of failing. By not being able to learn to read they had already failed. What they were afraid of is success.

Some years later, a group of schizophrenic patients brought this issue of the fear of success as compared to the fear of failure into even sharper focus for me.

For a number of years, I have taught a class in Family Life–Sex Education (a subject many professionals thought too volatile for the seriously disturbed) to groups of schizophrenic patients. One day in one of the classes we were talking about why people are afraid to form emotional relationships. I expected the answers to revolve around a fear of rejection, i.e., a fear of failure. However, the patients very clearly expressed a fear of *succeeding* in forming relationships, not a fear of *failing*. A fear of acceptance overshadowed a fear of rejection. They feared success because they felt their inadequacy would be revealed.

As one man said, "Once someone got to know me they'd see a big hole, an emptiness inside of me . . . and they'd leave."

Others in the class expressed the same feeling of unworthiness.

Later, I asked them how they felt when something good happened to them:

• When something good happens to me, I know I will have to pay for it.
• If something good happens to me, I try to reciprocate so that I don't lose the good thing.
• If things go well, I know someone or something will spoil it.
• When I feel it is too good, I know that I am the one who makes something bad happen.
• All my good dreams turn into nightmares. Feeling

bad is not strange; you get used to it. But feeling good. Wow.

No patients said that they felt terrific when something good happened to them. None of them felt entitled to success; their disturbed perception of self kept them from feeling deserving. They all had a fear of success.

Admittedly, these are seriously disturbed people. My point is that in this instance they are different only in degree from those of us who stay badly coupled, or stay in job situations that bore us, or live unrewarding, monotonous lives. Those of us who have a fear of success are as frightened of exposure as this class of schizophrenics, only just a little less so. And we're not afraid of failing. We've already failed. What we're afraid of is succeeding.

The acceptance of failure is a sure sign of the fear of success. Losers are people who fear winning.

Some of us may define success as something other people have and, thus, when we get it, all our problems of inadequacy, unworthiness, etcetera, will be solved. That success itself may be the problem never occurs to us. What we fail to notice is that much too often the only results of the success of others are anxiety, guilt, and a feeling of fraudulence, feelings that often lead to despair, retreat, depression, and that last stand, suicide.

It seems a source of mystery that the very goals we finally reach can be riddled with seeds of destruction. The mystery is cleared up when we realize that we've been carrying the seeds with us all along.

As we will see, those of us who have attained success can suffer from the fear of success every bit as much, and in some cases more, than those of us who are still striving. It all depends on what is going on in our psyches having to do with the subject of winning or losing, a subject that solidified for us in early childhood. To see where we stand on that matter, it's essential to find out how we fared in our Family Olympics.

3 /

Family Olympics I

The Oedipal Dilemma:

Beware of What You Want—

You May Get It

A YOUNG MOTHER put her five-year-old daughter out to die on the center divider of a busy California freeway. When the child was rescued, twelve hours later, her fingers had to be pried loose from the chain link fence.*

Few parents try to kill their children, and fewer still in such horrific ways. But the psychic damage parents unwittingly inflict upon their offspring can be every bit as damaging as actual physical violence.

There is no question that one of the best ways to avoid a fear of success is to start life with the right parents.

If I had my way, no two people would ever be al-

* This is one of the American horror stories reported by Joan Didion in The White Album (New York: Simon and Schuster, 1979).

37

lowed to create another human being, or raise one, without first taking and passing a course in Family Life–Sex Education.

People need to be taught how to be parents.

A woman said to me: "I had children. I gave them roots. Then I gave them wings."

In order to get roots and wings, children in early childhood need parental approval that is stripped of parental neuroticisms. Unfortunately, this is not an easy commodity to come by. Just because someone gets pregnant doesn't mean the parties responsible shed their unresolved psychological problems nine months later to greet the helpless newcomer as paragons of mental health. Too many parents are too emotionally immature to handle well the demands of child rearing. Good parenting does not come naturally. We are only now acknowledging that not everyone should be a parent. A mother who physically abuses her child does not hate the child—the mother hates her situation. And unless she resolves her situation, she will continue to abuse her child.

I am not just talking here of blood parents. I refer to anyone who is in charge of raising children—relatives, friends, strangers, the state—those people my profession calls significant others.

All need to understand, really understand, the sorts of interaction that can go on between family members. This is crucial to a child's upbringing, for it is as children within our families, or our surrogate families, that our future roles as adult competitors are determined. It is there, within the family dynamic, within, as I'll call it, the Family Olympics, that we are programmed for winning or losing, the groundwork either laid or not laid for a future fear of success.

A large majority of us emerge from this Olympics handicapped. Fortunately, the damage done is not necessarily permanent.

"The first thing I was taught to lose at home was an argument," said a young man who was in the process of destroying his career. He was on the verge of being bounced from his second job since graduating from law school a year before.

"My father, who thought he was entitled to a father-of-the-year award, never permitted me or my sister to challenge anything he said. He never hit us, but he picked a more deadly weapon—the silent treatment. It was not simply a matter of hours, but more like days before he would talk to me, and only after I had apologized profusely, which I would do when I could no longer tolerate his silence. Each time the silence started I felt he would never talk to me again and I was devastated. Ultimately, I stopped challenging him and then he started to tease me because of my passivity. It was a no-win situation.

"You never could have a joyous victory in our family. My father couldn't stand defeat. If I won a game of checkers or cards he didn't complain, he just didn't play with me anymore for a long time. It was a lonely victory. To avoid his withdrawal I learned not to win.

"There were times when the rage I felt for him would bubble up in me and I felt like killing him. I was awfully ashamed of these feelings, even though they were unspoken. I would sometimes transfer my anger to my mother, who was equally frightened by my father's silent treatment. I thought she should have protected me, but in retrospect I think she feared him more than I did.

"I've become the whipping boy of all the senior partners in my law firm. They're all out to get me. I don't mind being reprimanded by male superiors, but I can't tolerate being ignored. I bait them until they take me on; then I become anxious. For a long time I thought that the reason the other attorneys resented me was that I was the darling of most of the women in the office. I have a way with women. I guess I have a way with men, too, but it's usually destructive."

Indeed it is. If you grow up in a family, as this man did, where Father and/or Mother is always right and don't you forget it, don't you dare challenge them— "It's right because I said it's right"—your adult world is apt to be peopled with feared and hated Papa and Mama authority figures. And your life may be filled with power struggles that reenact the painful childhood situations that resulted from such destructive parental competition. If you've had overly punitive parents you may find yourself unable to work for a boss—any boss. If there has been hostile competition in the family, we can feel that our successes will bring out people's envy, anger, resentment, and even retaliation.

For this young man, becoming a lawyer meant being victorious over Dad because Dad was an insurance agent whose dream it had been to go to law school but his family had not had the resources. He wanted his son to fulfill him, yet never to surpass him. Winning over Dad, i.e., being a successful lawyer, signaled the silent treatment (abandonment). It was safer to lose. The moral of this tale is: How do you win in court if you've been trained to lose at home?

A young woman told me, "Whenever my family played Monopoly, it turned into World War III."

I would venture to say that most family inter-action sometimes resembles something like a world war—whether at the Monopoly board or not. What about your own family some evenings at the dinner table? (Remember, there can be cold, silent wars in addition to screaming conflagrations.)

A particularly aware female patient of mine told me, "When you come right down to it, we were a counterfeit family. We seemed to be very together, to have lots of positive mutuality. However, there was always a pervasive feeling that something was wrong; we just couldn't put our finger on it. When I hear that garbage about the family that prays together stays together, I could retch. We went to church (all six of us) every single Sunday of my life—until my father came on to me sexually. Instead of me telling on him, the bastard somehow made me think it was my fault. I was thirteen. He also threatened me if I told. Church never felt the same to me after that. And Daddy was not drunk when he did it; nor was he 'lower class.' At the time, he was an executive with a major corporation. And do you know what he threatened me with? If I told on him? He said he would sell my horse. Do you know what that means to a thirteen-year-old girl who lives only for horses!? I won't tell you what Daddy does today—but his picture's in *Newsweek* a whole lot. Our family was a sham."

Most of us who aren't mental health professionals

don't really know what goes on in families other than our own, and even with our own, if the pain has been too great, we wrap everything in myths and lies and secrets that take years to unscramble. Perfect dream families—those lovely Clarksons down the street—can be perfect nightmares in reality.

No family is without some conflict and anger. Whenever human beings group together, some friction of some sort is inevitable. And when the grouping is as close as family, the possibilities for distress are all too plentiful. A successful adult life has a better chance of developing in a family that is not ridden with unhealthy power struggles because of the inadequacies of those in charge.

We have defined the fear of success as not getting what you want because you feel you don't deserve it; now we will see that you think you don't deserve it because you feel guilty—about something. One of the very common things you can feel guilty about is to have won, when a child, the Oedipal sweepstakes. This is our first Family Olympic event, the parental triangle.

If you've never really taken the time to understand Freud's theory of the Oedipus complex, here's a bare bones, nontechnical explanation.

In Greek mythology Oedipus, the son of the king and queen of Thebes, was not raised by his parents but by the king of Corinth. When grown, he returned to Thebes and unwittingly killed his father and married his mother.

Yes, we're talking about incest.

Freud, who, among many other things, was a Greek

scholar of note, found in the Oedipus myth a good vehicle for his psychoanalytic theorizing. As used in psychoanalysis, the Oedipus complex is the unconscious tendency of a child to be attached to the parent of the opposite sex and hostile toward the other. A love triangle: father, mother, child. The child (at the age of five) wants one parent exclusively, but fears the anger of the other parent, whom the child also needs. Winning thus means losing, because of the expectation of anger and/or retaliation from the rival parent. It is not the frustration of not getting what we want that generates anxiety; it is the thought of successful acquisition that triggers it. Beware of what you want—you may get it.

I am not saying you actually want to have sex with Mommy or Daddy (although that is certainly within the realm of reality in some instances)—it's the *unconscious* incestuous wish that is the issue here.

The Oedipal competition, the first in our Family Olympics, is a natural occurrence, as is our second competition, that with siblings. It's only when parents, because of their own unresolved neurotic needs, unknowingly exacerbate the natural flow of these competitions that these normal phases do not resolve themselves in childhood but linger on, transforming themselves into adult conflicts. In the case of the Oedipal conflict, it is the carry-over into adulthood of guilt for unconscious incestuous wishes that is one pathway to the fear of success.

One of the damaging ways parents can interfere with normal competition is to urge a child to take sides in Mommy's and Daddy's warring relationship. The often said phrase "Who do you love better, your Mommy or your Daddy?" is not innocuous baby talk. It is dangerous. When parents don't fulfill each other they often use their children to fulfill themselves—both mothers and fathers. Thus we can have, e.g., Mommy and Son against that bastard Daddy or Daddy and Daughter against that shrew Mommy. Bastard and shrew are the parent's attitudes toward each other. Why drag in children for ballast?

Being called upon to mediate parental battles is an early lesson plan in how to lose. Whichever parent "wins," you lose. If you've sided with the "losing" parent, you automatically lose. If you've sided with the "winning" parent, you also lose—because you lose the "losing" parent and you feel guilty. As children, we cannot take sides without dire consequences; both parents carry our survival kits. A childhood fear of abandonment is terrifyingly concrete—e.g., Who will feed me? I'll starve. In classic role-playing marriages, the question for a child becomes, If I side with Daddy, and Mommy abandons me, who will cook the food for me? And if I side with Mommy, and Daddy abandons me, who will give Mommy the money to buy the food? Children are terribly helpless for a goodly number of years.

If one parent asks a child to side with him or her against the other, the child may be in trouble. An adult fear of success is more probable where there have been family coalitions, where the Olympic competition has been weighted. If a daughter is Daddy's favorite, she feels guilty for having usurped Mommy's "rightful" place and Mommy resents her. The same is true for a Mommy-son coalition. The seductive parent who woos the child instead of the mate destroys the normal competitive flow of things, throws a monkey wrench into the Family Olympics. The following young man had such a parent.

Rick, who is in his early twenties, is a rock singer who hit it very big about six months before I met him. Actually, he had hit it so big that he was experiencing what I call Instant Success Whiplash: his anxiety attacks were so massive he felt he could easily self-destruct.

At age twenty-two, Rick was making fantasylike amounts of money, and his adulation from fans was so great that it was sometimes physically dangerous. But he felt his live performances were "mostly shitty," and his recordings so flawed he couldn't listen to certain of the songs. The praise and money that flowed in simply made him shrug. His psyche knew he was not entitled to such success, even though his conscious self couldn't figure out why he was so miserable.

He said that each time he prepared for a performance or a recording session he banked on it being the "ultimate performance." Only then would he be all right—he would no longer feel so jumpy, so anxious, so discontented, so inadequate. Inevitably, no performance ever lived up to Rick's expectations. He was so obsessed with "performing" that he told me he hesitated in coming to see me because he was afraid he wouldn't give a good performance. I told him I wasn't in charge of any Top 10 chart and that this was one of the few places he could come and be a total mess.

It became clear fairly quickly that Rick was not

handling his overnight professional success at all well. And when we got to his emotional life, he revealed that in the last two years, since he was twenty, he had had five "serious" live-in lovers (not light affairs).

Rick had a definite fear of success. Here he was, about as "successful" as a young man in our contemporary culture can be, a rock idol, and his discontent was crippling him. As we talked, we discovered a number of things in his Family Olympics that, when taken together, had brought him to this anguished point of fearing success, both in his professional life and in his emotional life. One of the factors was undeniably an unresolved Oedipal dilemma.

Rick's father was a burly, macho, all-American Dad who ran a very successful big-time moving business. In his younger years, he had played pro ball—and he'd never forgotten one second of the experience. He wanted his son Rick who, by nature's wanton ways, had emerged small and frail and poorly put together for sports, not only to like sports, but to live for sports. Rick's earliest recall of a communication from Dad was, "Watch Petey! Why the hell don't you throw the ball like Petey!" (Petey lived two houses away and Petey, having emerged wiry and tough, was already a baby jock, the very opposite of his playmate Rick.) Rick hated sports. What he liked to do was sing and dance.

Rick's mother had been a showgirl before she married. The marriage had taken place when she and her husband had been in their youthful strutting prime. They had aged quickly, and badly, and as their showcase bodies began to sag, their attraction for each other had waned; there wasn't much left with which to connect. Pseudomutuality encased their marriage like a shroud.

Rick's parents didn't fight, but even worse sometimes than overt fighting—yelling, screaming, hitting, i.e., violent communication—is no communication at all. Parents can be at war, but a harsh word never is spoken. Pseudomutuality reigns. And children can sense the falsity. Rick's parents did not wish to solve their difficulties by divorcing. So, within the pretense of a good marriage, Rick's father had his beer, his televised sports, his successful business. And Rick's mother? Well, Rick's mother had Rick.

Rick could sing and dance all he wanted around Mom, the ex-showgirl. She encouraged him, approved of him, loved him. And thus unwittingly used him as a rebuke to her unloving husband.

Rick's father, before he grew to ignore—i.e., to reject—his son, tried to goad him into being the sort of son he wanted. He called Rick a sissy and a Mama's boy; he stopped short of calling him a homosexual, not out of any feeling for Rick, but because No Son of *Mine* Is a Goddamn Faggot. One summer Rick's father hired him to work in his warehouse. "It'll build you up," Dad said, "make a man of you." A few days after Rick started on the job, his father saw him sweating away lifting a heavy piece of furniture. He yelled out to him, "Drop it, kid; let the men handle it."

At one point in our talks, Rick said he felt like a fraud because he couldn't compete in the realm of regular people. I asked him what a realm of regular people consisted of. "Sports," he said. "The arts are for irregulars." Rick's Dad's messages had been powerful.

There was no way Rick could have pleased both his parents. He naturally gravitated to his mother and they became very close, one to the other. It's nice to go where one is approved of—even though with hindsight the loving experience can often be seen as one heavy with the possibility of psychic damage.

I feel that Rick's present-day frustration of longing for an "ultimate rock performance," one that he thinks would relieve him of his anxiety, that would make everything all right, translates into an unconscious incestuous wish. He cannot integrate and enjoy his success because, from this psychological perspective, success means having Mother—getting the parent you're not supposed to get, getting what you really are not supposed to have.

Fathers and mothers who have dealt with their own neurotic problems stand less of a chance of psychically injuring their children than do parents like Rick's. Rick's mother's need for love clamped itself on her son; thus she unintentionally used him as compensation for her unfulfilling marriage. And Rick's father was unable to rise above our culture's mighty approval of male sports bonding. If he had been able to give vent to his "softer" feelings, he might have been able to appreciate and love a skinny son who, although he couldn't catch a ball, could sing and dance with the best of 'em.

Parents must accept a child for who he is, not for who he could be for Mama or Papa. If the child cries a whole lot, that's who he is, a baby who cries a whole lot, *not* a baby who cries more than Johnny next door. And if Johnny next door walks before one's Billy, or says DaDa while Billy is still cooing, the parent's job is to accept Billy as he is, and not to expect him to walk before he walks or to talk before he talks. And so on down the whole long line of childhood learning. The child who gets love and acceptance for who he is, not for how well he compares to Johnny next door, stands the best chance of becoming a winner. In healthy competition, children should be striving to reach their personal potential; they should not be focusing their efforts on beating out others.

Lack of parental approval in early childhood almost invariably deposits one in the land of low self-esteem. Psychological rejection of a child because he does not fit a parent's mold is poor equipment for future success.

Freud put great stock in the Oedipal conflict as guilt maker, and thus cites it as an important factor in the fear of success. In "Those Wrecked by Success," he wrote:

> Psycho-analytic work teaches that the forces of conscience which induce illness on attainment of success, as in other cases on a frustration, are closely connected with the Oedipus-complex, the relation to father and mother, as perhaps, indeed, is all our sense of guilt in general.

I would add that guilt in relation to siblings, to brothers and sisters, can be every bit as crippling to the attainment of success as guilt in relation to Mom and Dad.

4 /

Family Olympics II

THE SIBLING DILEMMA:

I WANNA HAVE ALL THE CANDY

SIBLING RIVALRY, i.e., competition for parental approval between children living in the same family, is the second event in our Family Olympics and it, like our first competition, is full of possibilities for psychic havoc. Siblings do not have to be blood brothers and sisters. They can be the children of Mommy's new husband or Daddy's new wife, they can be your cousins who live with you, they can be the children in the orphanage where you grew up. Whoever they may be, guilt from an unresolved conflict with such siblings can be a stumbling block to success.

A frequent counterproductive parental message goes like this: Mother, putting her young son's or daughter's hand on her pregnant stomach and saying, "Just feel, darling, that's your new baby. You're just going to love your baby brother or sister."

Nonsense. Who could possibly love someone who takes away one's throne (even if it is only a high chair or a crib)? The child doesn't necessarily feel love for the new baby; he may feel threatened. Newly arrived sisters and brothers are not love objects; they are usually pains in the psyche.

What a predicament. Our parents insist that we love the newcomer, but we're filled with hate for the tiny squirming thing who takes up so much of Mommy's time. If only it would disappear, so that things could be as they were.

It's normal not to love the new competitor for our parents' attention; it's difficult to share love. In order to avoid our parents' displeasure, we learn to submerge our anger at our sibling. The repressed anger often comes out indirectly elsewhere—maybe we punch a kid down the street. And some of us strike out at the new baby when no one is looking. However, *we* know what we did. Guilt envelops us, though it may not emerge to harm us until years later. But emerge it will—unless our parents establish an atmosphere of nonhostile competition between offspring, and unless they stop all that propaganda about how much their current child is going to adore the new one.

The desperation children feel if a parent's approval goes to a sibling, whether the sibling is older or younger, is sometimes devastating. I'll never forget the desolation of the words of a woman who said: "I was always fighting with my older brother for my mother's attention. Mother had so little to give. If I lost it, I would have had nothing."

There has to be room within the family for sibling resentment to be acknowledged, not buried. And never brutally punished, physically or psychically, by humiliation or denigration. Some parents, in counterproductive fashion, demonstrate rage and even violence (e.g., slapping) against the child who is angry at the sibling, all in an effort to teach the angry child to behave lovingly to his brother or sister. What a confused lesson in loving!

A wise parent says, "I know you're angry at the new baby who isn't much fun and takes up a lot of my time. I understand why you don't like him and want to harm him. But he lives with us now; he's part of the family. I know you're unhappy, I understand you want to hurt him, but I cannot allow you to do that. It's okay to feel angry sometimes; you're not being bad for that. It's also okay *not* to feel angry about your baby brother. Sometimes he's even kinda cute."

Just as later, a wise parent says to a child who is screaming, "I wanna have all the candy. I don't wanna share with HER [his older sister]," "I understand you don't like to give up anything, but sometimes you have to share. And sometimes you don't have to share. It's all right not to share all the time."

Of course this all takes patience, infinite patience. How much easier to say, "Give your sister the candy before I belt you." If one is going to produce children, one had best be prepared for a lot of careful caretaking.

Brothers and sisters are a source of natural, normal competition. The competition becomes hostile if aided and abetted by parents. One of the worst ways in which parents can interfere is to demonstrate preference for one child over another. And I'm not just talking about the damage done to the child who feels *less* preferred; that's self-evident. I'm talking about those of us who were the apples of our parents' eyes.

If you were the preferred child, it may mean you were compared to your brothers and sisters and they lost. If parental approval rides on getting good school grades, for example, schoolwork is contaminated with undue anxiety. Because you want your parents' approval, success in school becomes imperative but, at the same time, because the success may represent the defeat of a sibling, it carries with it the taste of betrayal and a burden of guilt. From this perspective, success can be bittersweet indeed.

It certainly seems a paradox to end up feeling guilty because your parents approved of you! However, being approved of, i.e., feeling loved, is different from being preferred. In the sense we're talking of, love means: I love who you are. Preference means: I love you more than your sibling(s). Therefore your sister or brother got less love and approval because you got more. (As one of my students put it: "I usurped my mother's lap.") You took your parents' approval away from your sibling(s); they were deprived; they were rejected; they failed. And it's all your fault. You succeeded. You are guilty. And if you're guilty, you don't deserve to be successful. You have to mess up.

Preferred children frequently have an adult fear of success because they feel their success would repeat the hurt or destruction they perpetrated on brothers and sisters when all were young. Many of us do not succeed because we feel our success would destroy a sibling. For example:

A few years ago a twenty-eight-year-old man, Ernie, turned up in one of my Overcoming the Fear of Success classes. As usual, on the first day of class, students told why they had signed up for the course. Ernie said he had been trying to get his college degree for ten years now, but whenever he restarted he would pass only three out of four courses, get discouraged, and drop out. Another student suggested he take only three courses; maybe the work load was too heavy. "I did," he said, "and passed only two." I saw that Ernie was quite bright; obviously some psychological problem was stymieing his efforts at academic success.

Ernie had never given much thought to the psychological dynamics of his family; in fact it had been years since he had given much thought to his family, period, forget the dynamics. It had been a working-class family; Ernie had been the only one to finish high school. His older brother, who had been somewhat of a hell-raiser, had quit school as soon as it was legal to do so. Ernie had not seen this brother for ten years.

When class discussions began on how preferred children in a family often end up with a fear of success because they got all the goodies (parental approval), and thus feel guilty because their siblings were deprived, Ernie connected to the dynamic, even though he had never really known what sibling rivalry meant, and even though he had no idea he had been something called the preferred child. It floored him to think that maybe this was one of his problems. He had felt pride in the fact that his parents approved of his finishing school; he had liked being considered smarter than his brother; he had felt good when his mother had said, "Well, at least one of my sons is turning out okay." In no conscious way whatever did Ernie think he was hurting his brother. His brother didn't have it. So be it.

Late in the semester, when Ernie had looked deeper into the preferred child syndrome, he tracked down his brother. He had expected to find a poor, miserable guy, maybe even someone in trouble with the law. What he found was a brother who was a plumber, who was doing well on his job, who liked his work, and who had just bought himself a silver sports car he had coveted for several years. Ernie's brother was doing all right; in fact, relatively speaking, he was doing much better than Ernie. There was no doubt he felt he deserved success.

Ernie's academic frustrations had come out of an unconscious need to be unsuccessful, as he thought his brother surely was, so that he needn't feel guilty for having won over him in childhood. If they were *both* adult failures, Ernie would be absolved of having been a bad person.

Seeing his brother in such good shape made an impact on Ernie. By the end of the semester, it was clear to me that he was now better equipped to overcome his fear of success on the academic scene. He had discovered an underlying dynamic that had been blocking him. Maybe he would be able to work through that sibling conflict and pass that last course; maybe he would go on to discover other blocks. Whatever happened, one thing was certain: he would not again be repeating a pattern that failed and wondering yet again what in the world had gone wrong.

Brett, a woman who is as beautiful as she is intelligent but who "just can't get it together," spent the first few years of her life being, as she tells it, "loved to pieces" by her parents. She was the adored child because she was the only child. Then: enter new baby— a brother—brain-damaged. Suddenly, Brett's childhood accomplishments, for which she once had received praise, were now discouraged. But more painful than the discouragement of what she already knew was the indifference on the part of her parents when she accomplished some new childhood task. "Don't show off in front of your brother," her mother would say. "You know he can't do that." Thus, being competent at something came to mean "showing off"; competence did not bring parental approval.

Brett was never allowed to enjoy her successes; they became things to hide. She no longer was the adored child. She came to resent her brother and feel little compassion for his handicapped state.

Family life was one long sadness. Her mother's litany was: "We could have been a happy family if we didn't have this tragedy," i.e., this retarded brother. As a child, Brett translated her mother's words as: "If brother died, we'd be a happy family." She thought, Why doesn't he die? I wish he *would* die.

A few years later, the brother, whose name was Daniel, did die. After the death, the family did not, as the mother had predicted, become happy. And Brett, the surviving offspring, was left with terrible feelings of guilt ("my wish for his death came true") and, later in life, an adult fear of success. In her mind a killer did not deserve success.

No one in his right mind would say that it is easy to cope with the trauma of producing a brain-damaged child. Many parents are able to handle the trauma but some enter shell shock and some never emerge. As for the effect on siblings, it can be disastrous. It is often a no-win situation. If parents prefer the non-brain-damaged child, this child may go through all the problems of the preferred child. And if the parents, out of problems of their own, prefer the handicapped child, psychological damage to the other child is predictable.

What's called for is a realistic approach on the part of parents, a concentration on not showing preference for one child, but accepting both for exactly who they are. What's needed is a guilt-free look at the situation, as in the case of Brett and Daniel: Daniel is handicapped; there are certain things he can do and for those things he will get our encouragement and approval and love. Brett is not handicapped; she can do many things. For them she will get our encouragement and approval and love. Yes, of course, stiff upper lip aside, having a brain-damaged child may well be a tragedy—but we will not slide into a life dictated by the joy of suffering. We will not use Daniel as an excuse for all our problems. And we certainly will not sacrifice our daughter's potential in a misguided attempt to make life happier for our handicapped son.

One of the terrible trials of childhood is the almost universal feeling on the part of youngsters that they are to blame for any and all of the family trouble. From their self-centered world they think, I've been bad; it's my fault; I'm to blame. Recent studies of children of divorce and children of alcoholics show this very clearly.

A nine-year-old girl of divorced parents: "In a way, I thought I'd made [the divorce] happen. I thought maybe I'd acted mean to my mother and my sister and I was being punished by God."

A ten-year-old boy whose mother is alcoholic: "Sorta got guilty, like I made her drink cause I talked back. Sorta like if I would of been good, she would of been better."*

It's all my fault. I'm responsible. I'm the bad person. I'm guilty. And if I'm guilty, I'm not worthy of success in life.

By far the most crippling feeling of guilt we can harbor is that of thinking we have caused the death of a parent. This is especially true if the feeling has stemmed from the age of five or six, when we were going through the traumatic Oedipal phase.

During this period, when children are competing with one parent for the other, it's quite common for them to have murderous wishes toward the rival parent. Why doesn't he/she just die? they think. For children, being dead means for five minutes or for an hour. In one way or another we all had such wishes as children. The guilt that can result from simply wanting the rival parent out of the triangle is devastating; just imagine if

* Both quotes are from *Newsweek*, February 11, 1980, and May 28, 1979.

the rival actually should die. In the child's unconscious the parent's death means the child has won—but what a victory! Any further effort at winning (i.e., success) in life is a losing battle. The same goes for having wished for the death of a sibling who subsequently dies.

If a child reaches adulthood with the unresolved feeling of having caused the death of a parent or sibling, a fear of success is predictable. Other childhood factors that contribute to a fear of success, including an unresolved Oedipal conflict or a sibling conflict, are usually cumulative, but a feeling that one has killed Mommy or Daddy or sister or brother needs no supporting factors. The guilt is just too crippling. Children must be taught that murderous wishes do not come true. Parents and siblings do not die because we will it.

In dealing with childhood competition both during the Oedipal phase and during conflicts with siblings, it's important to create a family atmosphere in which the expression of anger is comfortably encompassed and not harshly censored. Otherwise, the angry child is bound to feel like a monster. And in his childhood bedside reading, monsters always lose; they do not become successful.

As we grow, in acts of assertion we may refight the parental and/or sibling battles. If these original competitions have been conducted in an atmosphere of hostility, we enter the new competitions (school, jobs, loves) with a handicap; if the hostility has been too severe, we may not bother to enter at all. We may be so frightened of a possible psychic injury, e.g., rejection or humiliation, that we don't attempt to win, we don't attempt to be successful. We repress our anger and we develop an inhibition of aggression. The psychic energy it takes to deny our angry feelings is at the expense of the energy needed for the creative effort to be successful in our work lives and in our love lives.

Aggression is usually seen as a hostile wish to dominate, but in its positive sense it means to do, to move, to create, to succeed. The inhibition of this sort of aggression is a major symptom of the fear of success.

If we have been handicapped in our Family Olympics, if we are fired by ambition but blocked by the fear of retaliation for our Oedipal and sibling guilts, any act of assertion may mean we are attacking others. Thus we develop a fear of success that manifests itself in performance anxiety. If we have weathered our Family Olympics relatively intact, our assertive behavior simply means we are using our initiative and enterprise effectively. We are hurting no one when we advance ourselves.

Performance anxiety can be defined as that uneasy feeling we have prior to or during some event. The unconscious question is: How will I perform or how am I performing? Students may have it before an exam or they may go blank during one. Actors may forget their lines. Singers may lose their voices. Lovers may be unable to reach orgasm. The anxiety that blocks us may be mild or it may be paralyzing. It depends largely on what went on in our Family Olympics.

A psychologically oriented young actress told me that when she reads for an understudy role she is without anxiety and always gets the job. "If I know a star is slated to play the role," she said, "it seems to take the danger out of daring to think I could play it. The star is the safety valve; she gives me a freedom I don't have when I read for performing roles." Conversant with the theory of the fear of success, she went on to say, "In my family I was the leading lady. My mother and sister played cameo roles. Perhaps not shining in my career is the price I have to pay for my childhood winning."

Understudies usually wish to play the role, but they couch their desire by saying, "Not that I wish anything bad would happen to so-and-so," whereas unconsciously they damn well may wish something bad would happen to so-and-so. Is this not an echo of a childhood wish to replace a parent or sibling? Is it not an echo of the cultural adage "One man's gain, another man's sorrow?" Therein lies the conflict and therein lies the guilt. Performance anxiety under such circumstances is predictable.

Performance anxiety may occur when we observe ourselves having sex. This is another area where we may encounter the fear of success. From sex therapists come numerous stories of a sexually dysfunctional partner, a premature ejaculator (one such man told his therapist, "I don't give a fuck!"), an impotent man, a nonorgasmic woman. When a dysfunctional partner becomes functional, the other partner may go into a depression. Incomprehensible as it may seem, he or she goes off on a long trip, starts staying late at the office, or even suggests a separation. The latent contract in the relationship may have been: the less sex, the better; the quicker, the better.

Most people in our culture have been programmed not to have sex too soon, too often, or too late in life.

In other words, don't reap too many rewards and don't enjoy yourself too much. Too much pleasure certainly will turn into grief. When good things are suspect and bad things inevitable it is safe to wager that a fear of success is at the bottom of things.

For some the only tolerable coping mechanism for performance anxiety is to drop out. Playwrights have disappeared on opening night. Students have dropped out of school, and some out of society. People drop out by falling into a stupor called depression. Some call it apathy. Apathy is a paralysis of movement, for to move may mean to assert, and assertion, as we have seen, may bring reprisal.

The most extreme way of dropping out is to commit suicide after having achieved public acclaim. Kill themselves when their goal has been achieved? It seems incomprehensible. Surely they must have learned they had a terminal illness. No. The illness is a fear of success.

5 /

Family Olympics III

MESSAGES: THE CRITICS IN OUR LIVES

THE MANNER in which we respond to negative criticism is a clue to the level of our self-esteem, which in turn is a good index to the degree of our fear of success. If we harbor a feeling of inadequacy, as many of us do, about something, no matter how slight, negative criticism can wipe us out. Most of us carry with us too many internalized low-esteem messages from the past, negative things our parents or siblings or teachers or schoolday peers said to us. Even one negative remark may trigger any one of these messages, leading us to feel rampant self-doubt about our competency. Even though there may be bouquets of praise around, that one remark is zeroed in on and attended to as if nothing else were said.

Few of us are without self-doubt. Not too long ago, an officer of the law stopped my car. I immediately had a mild anxiety attack. A cop stopping my car meant I was in for negative criticism. All it turned out to be was an unhinged license plate, but all of my self-doubt of the past had come rushing forth, completely overshadowing the fact that I hadn't done anything wrong and in fact was not a bad example of an upstanding citizen.

How we handle negative criticism or the threat of negative criticism in our adult lives correlates with the ego strength we developed in the interaction with our very first and most important critics, our parents or surrogates. From the day we are born we receive good or bad reviews from these first critics. If there are more good notices than bad, it will be easier to deal with negative criticism when we're grown. Even though we stow away all of the reviews, good and bad, we internalize more of the negatives than the positives. As children, we're taught Don't before we're taught Do.

When I ask people what they recall as commendations from parents, they usually draw a blank. When I ask them about negative parental criticism they could talk for hours. Some of our parents' favorite one-liners go like this:

You have a way of always doing the wrong thing at the right time.

You owe it all to me.

Do the best you can (which may not be much).

If only I had your advantages.

You're too smart for your own good.

You'll end up like your uncle, a bum.

If it weren't for you, I could have lived in beauty . . .
   I could have been a great artist . . .
What did I do to deserve you?
You'll be the death of me.
Do whatever you want, but make me proud.
Don't be a show-off.
You don't know when you are well off.
Don't upset Mom; you know she's high-strung.
Lower your voice when you talk to me.
How come you always call your friends and they never
   call you?
Are you staying home again tonight?
You got that from my side of the family (good). You
   got that from her/his side of the family (bad).
There's absolutely nothing in this world you can't do
   if you just apply yourself.
You have a face only a mother could love.
If you can do it, it's no big deal.

Christopher, a man who as a high school student
watched a lot of television, got the following verbal
message from his parents: "Would you please turn off
your goddamn TV? Why can't you be like your cousin
Mark? He's so busy studying he doesn't have time for
TV."

That was the verbal message. Here's what Christopher internalized: Your cousin Mark will grow up to
have a great career while you, our son, our inadequate
son, will wind up on the garbage heap with faulty

vision. As a result, Christopher's motivation for success became based on revenge, on a wish to get even with these parents who were predicting doom for him. And, at the age of thirty-two, Christopher did achieve some measure of external success. He had become a TV producer of note.

Today, Christopher says, "You see, I proved my parents wrong. They predicted I'd fall on my ass and look, I'm a huge fucking success. I showed them."

Even though Christopher had just won an industry-wide award when he said this, the words are sheer bravura. Christopher is not a success. He's an anxiety-ridden mess. He drinks too much, he smokes too much, his fingernails barely exist. He suffers periodically from colitis and he's never had a satisfying emotional relationship with anyone. In addition, he can't move out of the dingy but cheap walk-up apartment he moved into when he first was starting out in TV land—even though he's been mugged twice. "What if I lose my job?" he asks. "Who can pay New York rents these days?"

Someone who has an underlying feeling of inadequacy like Christopher is often inordinately afraid of losing his job. Someone who does not have a fear of success does not spend most of his time worrying about losing his job.

Christopher's anxiety does not stem from the well-acknowledged pressures of the television industry. His anxiety is prompted by his internal fury for all the negative criticism his parents communicated to him, all the while telling him it was for his own good that they harassed him. Christopher's drive for success is based on taking revenge for those hurts, and in this way he is still responding to the inadequacy messages of his parents. Until he works through his anger toward his parents, he will continue to be the anxiety-ridden man that he is—even if his entire living room is filled with television merit awards.

Christopher's good cousin Mark, he who never had watched TV, did not fare much better than Christopher on the fear-of-success scale, although he did fare differently. After high school, Mark had taken over his father's business and had gone bankrupt. A goody-two-shoes-child can also grow up to have a fear of success.

Good cousin Mark had his own family dynamics with which to cope; when a youngster in our culture never watches TV, something has to be up. It's often, as it was in Mark's case, a matter of overcontrolling parents. While growing up, Mark was seriously deprived of pleasurable activities. No television was just one rule in a long list. From the day he was born, Mark was groomed to take over his father's business, and business being a serious matter, normal childhood pleasures such as occasionally goofing off were strictly forbidden. Mark was not born a goody-two-shoes child; because of his controlling parents he knew that his life depended on staying in the role of being supergood. Everything in life save his father's business was made to seem peripheral to him. Any desire of his to be "bad," i.e., to enjoy or even be interested in other things life had to offer, produced a terrible feeling of guilt. The rage he felt for his autocratic parents was enormous, but he suppressed it.

Eventually, Mark got his revenge by ruining his father's business. In this way, he also hurt himself, but there was nowhere else that his sublimated rage, when it surfaced, could go. Mark had never wanted Dad's business, but because his role was that of the good, obedient child, because he had been programmed so, he did not make his real feelings known and thus ended by sabotaging himself.

I can't repeat this often enough: success based on anything save internal fulfillment is bound to ring hollow, if not today, then tomorrow. Sometimes, as in the case of a young medical intern named Charlie, it may prove to be dangerous.

Charlie's tyrannical father always minimized his son's achievements by saying to him, "Some people have it and some don't." Charlie knew from an early age that this parental message meant that he, Charlie, didn't have it. Yet, on his deathbed, this father said to his "loser" son, "I want you to promise me you will become a doctor."

There is nothing basically sacred about the wishes of dying people. The act of dying does not necessarily give the ill greater wisdom. The dying may elicit feelings of sadness or anger or relief, we may or may not mourn them, but we are not obliged to execute their deathbed plans for us. (Many who mourn endlessly do so more out of guilt than out of legitimate anguish.) Deathbed promises make for good drama, but they are best left to fiction. Far too many real life pledges have been carried out to the detriment of the pledger—and sometimes to others.

Charlie, although he had no real interest in medicine, couldn't disappoint his father. He finally had the approval he always wanted. To be a doctor you had to have "it." Come what may, Charlie would be a doctor. He enrolled in college and started the long road to an M.D. degree.

In college he barely managed to pass his premed courses. He didn't like science; chemistry and physics were a torture. He invested the money he earned part-time in a tutor, and managed to squeak through. He did not get into a medical school in the United States, so he went abroad. He was always on the verge of dropping out of the foreign school, but he kept hearing his father's deathbed voice. After six years, he managed to finish.

Charlie now has an internship in a second-rate U.S. hospital where he indeed may become a second-rate doctor. There is every possibility that his father's dying words may put Charlie—and others—in jeopardy.

Given a free choice of career, Charlie would have chosen social work. Being in a helping profession is not at all alien to him. But to please his father he ignored his own feelings. It is only when Charlie realizes that his father's dying words were not words of support that he will be able to come to terms with who he really is, rather than continue to be what a misguided father now long dead wanted him to be.

In some cases, dying people such as Charlie's father who extract promises that their will be done are on an ultimate power trip. Just because people are in the process of dying, this extremely common act does not absolve them of whatever living neuroses they may have had.

This is a good point to bring up something that has bothered me for some time: Why is the career of medicine endowed with such godlike qualities? Even the most marvelous and intelligent of beings get all fluttery on the subject. One such marvelous and intelligent woman, a pediatrician who became a child psychiatrist, said she believed that the only profession worthy of dignity was medicine. I challenged her bias. She wouldn't budge on the subject, but she could laugh at herself. She told me the following joke:

"I went to a gathering of all my children and grandchildren and they gave me a seat of prominence in their circle. One by one I asked each grandchild what he or she wanted to be when he or she grew up. 'Fireman,' one said, predictably. Others chimed in: 'jet pilot' (this from a girl child; times had changed); 'a mother' (this from the jet pilot's younger sister; times had not changed all that much); President of the United States of America, and so on.

" 'Wonderful,' I said, 'terrific . . . but first go to medical school.' "

Some children receive negative parental reviews for every act. Others get raves for every act, praise that has little to do with actual performance. Neither parental attitude is conducive to good mental health. What's needed is an atmosphere where parents encourage growth by giving an appropriate amount of positive support. Only then can criticism in later life be met with realistic appraisal.

For those of us who spent our childhoods trying to ward off a steady stream of harsh criticism, the damage may have been so great that we always play it safe, never venturing into any sort of limelight, never getting involved in anything. This guarantees a life free of negative criticism. There are no risks, but neither is there true satisfaction—a life of quietly sitting at home not fulfilling oneself is a clear-cut example of the fear of success.

Others of us, even though equally victimized by destructive criticism in early childhood, relish returning to the scene of the crime, as victims.

There are many avenues by which we can return to the scene of the crime. Some of us take the path that guarantees rejection. We are drawn to people who are not interested in us, or to those who actively renounce us. We believe that these are the only people who hold the key to our happiness and, since these people are unattainable, we must suffer the pangs of frustration. Those who respond favorably to us are generally less than adequate. It's the lack of availability that spurs us on.

"It has the flavor of mother's milk," says a superficially savvy young woman about being rejected by a man she cares about. "It almost has a taste of sour milk that is not repugnant to me. All sorts of body fluids are activated by my being unwanted. I soak in the sweat of anxiety. I drench myself in tears, and I salivate with a desire for a sweet to compensate for my anguish. Those sweets are temporary sources of relief; the anxiety generated by the consumption of the sweets which expands my waistline reactivates the tear ducts."

Her parents' rejection of her ("You're more trouble than you're worth") is early pain that is revitalized when she pursues a lover who from the onset cues her that any genuine intimacy is anathema to him. She thinks she wants to be with someone who is as eager for human contact as she is, but she rarely finds such a relationship, so she holds herself suspect because she is a champion at finding the elusive. Total acceptance in a relationship is alien to her.

She says, "I don't know what to do with unequivocal love. I don't trust it. I don't think I deserve it. My parents never loved me. They thought I was worthless, and if they thought so, it must have been true."

Clearly, negative parental messages carry enormous weight. It is this sort of communication that first establishes our attitudes about our self-worth. And if this attitude is more negative than positive, a fear of success, that is, a life of self-sabotage in the adult worlds of work and love, is predictable.

After we have internalized the messages of our parents and siblings, we move on to our second set of critics, our teachers, those whose job it is to further program us for success or failure by branding us with letters that run from A to F.

I feel that too much rides on childhood report cards; it's a rating system that can prove most injurious. It is enough for a student to know if he's written right answers or wrong answers. And enough for a teacher to know if the student understands what he has written. Those students who flourish despite bad report cards, a minority, usually have especially supportive parents. For the rest of us, school ratings have an important effect on our self-esteem.

Even if teachers try to soften the blow by, for example, calling reading groups Bluebirds, Robins, and Sparrows, children know. They know that Bluebirds are the smartest, Robins okay, and Sparrows dumb. Many a bright child has worn the plumage of a dumb bird and has gone through life with this damaged self-concept.

Tragic experiences have resulted from school days, when we were too young and didn't have the psychic tools with which to fight back. If a teacher says to a child, "You're a dummy," the child is usually going to believe it. This is especially true if his first set of critics, his parents, have been destructively critical toward him. To him, the teacher's remark is one more humiliation.

Just as the motivation of some people for success is based on getting even with parents, as in the just-related case of Christopher, so too do some people vow to get even with teachers. A Sparrow (or a dummy) can spend a better part of his life trying to prove a teacher as well as a parent wrong. He may seek power-structure positions so that no one will be in a position to humiliate him ever again. Sparrow, indeed. He may become a hawk.

Harvey is a hawk. At fifty he runs a giant conglomerate that has made him a multimillionaire superpower. Harvey does not compete to win but to get even. His entire existence depends upon outdistancing others. He waits in prey for anyone in his path and wipes them out with little compunction. This he designates as a reasonable design for living; if he doesn't keep his guard up, someone might discover that he once was a Sparrow.

As a son and as a student, Harvey was thought to be a flop. Ignored by parents who found him inconvenient, Harvey's father's response to most of his statements was, "It's only your opinion." Harvey's reading of that was, I am invalid. He clearly developed a poor opinion of himself. He became what his teachers in their annual report referred to as a behavior problem. He didn't do anything dramatically offbeat but he sometimes refused to answer questions when called upon, especially if he didn't know the answer; he knew the art of cover-up before it became a national ploy. Teachers were on to him. They didn't like him and he seemed not to care.

But pained and humiliated, Harvey vowed to get even. He buried his feelings for others and, with a single-mindedness that precluded pleasurable activities, he set out to control his environment by amassing huge amounts of money which he equated with power. He manipulated and exploited his way to chairman of the board. Not once did he let compassion for others deter him. He eliminated it from his repertoire of feelings. His relentless quest for power elicited hatred, which he interpreted as an indication of the success of his strategy (they hate me because I am doing better than they are). Anyone who did not pursue money as he did was just plain dumb. Thus he converted teachers into inferior creatures because they worked for so little remuneration. It was at long last Harvey's turn to call all teachers dummy. Unlike those of us who have an inhibition of aggression, fearing competition lest we induce anger in others, Harvey is aggressive to a fault, acting out his rage toward his parents and his teachers.

You may be thinking, Well, the man *is* a success; what he does affects thousands; he is powerful and he seems to have achieved his carefully planned campaign for success. Do negative messages from parents and teachers spur us on to positive results? No, not really. Harvey is not powerful; he is frail. He is posturing. He has never truly dealt with past humiliation and pain. It's always with him, unresolved. Once off guard, he fears he might be humiliated again so he builds barriers between himself and others; he particularly avoids acts of intimacy. Recently he had his gall bladder removed, a possible index to inner chaos. During the recuperative period, he realized his vulnerability. He contemplates getting professional help for the bouts of anxiety he is beginning to experience, but fears it would make *him* prey to birds of another feather.

Do some teachers really call pupils dumb? Yes. And worse. Inspirational teachers are not all that common. If you find any, honor them. For the most part, our elementary school teachers are not the cream of our crop. We don't pay them enough, nor do we give them enough respect. And the demands we place upon them are so heavy that many try to get by without too much investment. Some hardly listen to their charges. Example:

Teacher: And how did you spend your summer, children?

Pupil: We went to the Amish country. [This interchange happened in a wealthy New York suburb where parents view a summer holiday as an opportunity for a seminar in anthropology, the better to get into Harvard.] And my father was so interested in the clothes that the Amish people wear that he backed his car into a fence and smashed his fender.

Teacher: That's *very* nice, dear. Next.

From teachers we go on to face employers, colleagues, friends, lovers, spouses and, some of us, professional critics and the public. How we react to negative criticism from these additional critics in our lives very much depends upon the quality of those internalized parental, sibling, teacher, and peer communications, those very first reviews we got, now so carefully stowed away in our psychic knapsacks.

There are those of us who have to face professional critics. Writers, for example.

I have yet to meet a writer, a writer of fiction, who does not come to understand the fear of success. Anyone who reveals family secrets, and so publicly, is bound, at one time or another, to have a brush with the malady. A writer's block is often a symptom of the fear of success.

I have always felt that writers may be prone to the joy of suffering. Take, for example, the fact that many live their lives facing a series of deadlines. The word itself is frightening: dead line. It comes from a marked-out line that ran along and inside of the peripheral fence of the Confederate prisoner-of-war camp, Andersonville. A prisoner crossing this line was shot. It was a dead line.

However, many writers finish books before the deadline. Then, for those who have internalized negative messages from the past, comes the agony of publication day. Some leave the country to avoid the reviews; some leave in a stupor of alcohol; some walk around like zombies; others operate in a state of mania. Some escape into physical illness. Thus the accomplishment of the goal arduously pursued produces terror.

Writers have described the pleasures of writing, the

loneliness of writing, the drudgery of writing—all tolerable feelings. The real anxiety for some comes when it's time for reviews. To them, even good reviews don't sound authentic; bad ones prove their deepest suspicions of fraudulence and inadequacy. They have been found out. Exposed. Dwelling on negative criticism and trying to please the critics next time around can lead to paralysis of effort—and no next time. Only those who have uprooted damaging parental, sibling, teacher, and peer communications can meet negative criticism with realistic appraisal, instead of having it trigger self-doubt. This is true for all of us, not only for those who must face professional critics.

Friction between colleagues on the job has affected all of us at one time or another. There is little doubt that being well-liked at work makes the job more agreeable. But in order to guarantee our own psychic health we must choose competency over being well-liked. And often, this in itself—if your antagonistic colleague's psyche is in good order—will lead to being well liked.

One of my most exciting jobs was in an experimental therapeutic community of outpatient schizophrenics. (This work is not the same as the clinic work with schizophrenics I describe elsewhere.) When I started working in this experimental program, I wasn't all that well liked by some members of the staff. I've always been a maverick in my work, using blunt talk and humor, and most of it noisy, as my therapeutic tools, especially with those seriously disturbed people who are difficult to reach. Sometimes I get carried away with my humor, and sometimes my interpretations are a little too far out for my more conservative colleagues. At times, I am called too Freudian, at other times too aggressively non-Freudian.

In the therapeutic community, there was a staff psychiatrist who had her office next to mine. She was a quiet, polite, gentle, dignified person who did an excellent job nurturing her patients. Compared to her, I was like a bull in a china shop; I joked with, yelled at, teased, and provoked my patients—all in an effort to reach them. If, for example, I said to a patient, "Knock off the bullshit" (what Freudian would ever do that!), it was meant to convey to him that he had strengths underneath the cover-up.

One day, this psychiatrist—let's call her Mary—could, I suppose, no longer stand it. She came into my office and said, "Frieda Fromm-Reichmann is turning over in her grave! Nobody talks to patients that way. Nobody says to them, 'How did you get so fucked up?'" (Today I have private patients who talk to *me* that way; not long ago I offered a long and intricate interpretation to a woman about an area of her life she had been holding forth on all session. She listened, but when I finished she looked at me and said, with tongue in cheek, "What the fuck do *you* know about this?")

My quiet colleague Mary went on to call me an aggressive show-off. Talk about triggering childhood negative messages! Show-off. Putting on an act. Performing for Daddy. As you will see shortly, when I discuss my own fear of success, I had a good deal of trouble with my self-concept revolving around performing for Daddy. It had taken me years to come to terms with all that childhood damage. But I *had* come to terms with it. So when Mary's remark about my being a show-off began, because of internalized negative messages, to trigger self-doubt, I was able to see what was happening and to stop it before it got out of hand. Eventually, not immediately, but eventually, I was able to approach Mary and say, "Let's talk." And we did, not only about negative feelings about each other, but about positive feelings.

We both prospered by our talks. She invited me to become a co-therapist and together we did some terrific (if I do say so) family therapy. She had skills I didn't have and I had skills she didn't have; the families we treated had the benefits of both. Some on the staff insisted that co-therapists should be of opposite sexes so that they could be male/female role models for the patients. Mary and I answered, "It's best to have two *good* family therapists."

I stayed in that job ten years. I worked hard, I developed more skills, I became more competent, I gained respect. Of course, not everyone on staff liked me, but that's not the goal. The goal is competency. I no longer mind being called a show-off, a joker, a performer. It has taken years, but I've turned that childhood damage around. Those words now mean that I'm a pretty funny woman—and that sits just fine with me. I now look upon it as a personality strength . . . at least most of the time. And for us frail human beings, most of the time is a far sight better than none of the time.

All right, you may be saying, you and Mary were therapists, your very jobs made you receptive to solving your friction. What about solving colleague friction between people who aren't psychologically oriented?

First of all, you wouldn't be reading this book if you weren't psychologically curious. I would advise: talk. Talking about feelings is a first step toward easing tensions, even if at first it's just a venting of anger. Even large corporations have seen the value of organized sensitivity training sessions where employees can talk about job feelings rather than just productivity rates.

I would also advise you to look very hard at the job itself. If it is something you really like doing, just continue to go about your business, striving for competency. Not everyone will like and respect you, but who ever wins over everyone? If *your* psyche is in good order, the chances are that the psyches of those who don't like you would benefit from some exploration. And that's not *your* problem.

If your psyche is not in good order, if present-day negative criticism triggers your internalized parental, sibling, teacher, or peer put-downs, making you feel inadequate, you must stop living with a Band-Aid holding together your mental well-being and start exploring and rebuilding.

In dealing with negative criticism, the need to be competent must overshadow the need to be well-liked. Is it worthwhile to bend over backward for approval if in the process your self-fulfillment is sabotaged . . . or, for some of us, societal progress is thwarted?

What would the status of women be today if Alice Paul and her contemporary feminists hadn't risked the jeers, the insults, and even being spat upon when they marched in Washington in 1913 for women's suffrage? These women were not much liked. Nor are their present-day counterparts who are demanding to be included in the Constitution via the Equal Rights Amendment.

How would most of our elderly live today if the original advocates of our Social Security system had kowtowed to avoid being labeled Communists? These people weren't much liked either.

Our country would be in much worse shape than it is if pioneers for social change were less concerned with truth and competency and more concerned with being well-liked. Whatever other psychological problems they may have had, these pioneers were able to integrate the name-calling. They were able to deal with the critics in their lives.

6 /

A Little White Lie Here,
One There

It's the rare person who feels totally honest with himself. Most of us hold tight to some sort of secret we don't want revealed, something in our past that makes us feel fraudulent in the here and now, some sort of skeleton in the closet—whether real or make-believe, whether trivial or tragic. The fear of exposure that results from such hiding is a sure sign of the fear of success. The fear can be mild and not terribly life-disrupting, as in the first case reported below, or it can be severe and life-destroying, as in the second case.

#1: The Most Fortunate Man in the World

I have a colleague who, at the time of this writing, was about to marry a man who is a financial wizard. It was to be a second marriage for both.

One evening while visiting with Marlene and Gerald, talk turned to what I was working on—the writing of this book about the fear of success. Marlene is very tuned in to the theory, finds it helpful in her practice, but Gerald, like most lay people, had never given the concept much thought.

Gerald is a self-made man. In classic American free enterprise tradition he created a phenomenal success of a business that he started with one small retail shop. Just two weeks earlier, the *Wall Street Journal* had run a feature article about him and his famous business.

I asked this very successful businessman if he felt at all uneasy with such success. He said, no, that now, finally, after years filled with obstacles, he wasn't conscious of any unease. He felt very successful—on all fronts.

Marlene raised her eyebrows. "Tell Martha about your dream," she said.

Gerald hesitated.

"Come on," Marlene said. "If you're going to marry me you've got to start tuning in to all this Viennese Voodoo.* Maybe together Martha and I can make some sense of it. Who knows—it might even give her a case for her book."

We all laughed.

Gerald said, "All right, what the hell. You see, I was invited to the White House . . ."

Marlene interrupted. "First tell her all that happened on the *day* of the night you had the dream."

---

* "Viennese Voodoo" is not original with my colleague Marlene. It's what the critic John Leonard said Nabokov would have called psychiatry. *The New York Times*, November 30, 1979.

It seems that when the *Wall Street Journal* article appeared, instead of feeling elated, Gerald had had mixed feelings. He had had a tumor removed and was awaiting the results of the biopsy. He felt his life was quite likely in jeopardy. That afternoon he learned that the tumor was benign. Later that day, his company hit a new high on the stock market, and that evening he asked Marlene to marry him and she agreed. Gerald said he felt that that day he was the most fortunate man in the world; he thought he now had everything.

That night he had his dream.

"I was invited to the White House by the President of the United States; he escorted me through each room. He was a rather heavyset man with a nice smile. He said he wanted to have a high-level conference with me and recommended that we confer at the top of the Washington Monument. He said I would be propelled upward in a chair that would be operated by a motor. I looked frightened and he tried to reassure me. 'Don't worry,' he said. 'We will strap you into the chair.' Feeling fearful of that height, I asked, 'Why can't I take an elevator?' There was no real answer.

"Later the President motioned to me and pointed to two horses. I relaxed. I mounted a horse and felt comfortable on it because I felt it was really a bicycle. It was a bicycle that was shaped like a horse. I felt comfortable sitting on the bicycle . . . but I felt great anxiety about climbing to the top of the Washington Monument to confer with the President.

"I couldn't do it."

In talking, Gerald revealed that while he was growing up his father owned an unsuccessful bicycle shop.

Marlene and I agreed that the dream probably illustrated Gerald's fear of surpassing Father. He felt safe on the ground, on the bicycle, on the same level as his father, but he felt he could not reach higher, even though the President—the father of the country—tried to elevate him—and securely.

Gerald was amazed by his dream and it took several go-arounds before he accepted our interpretation.

"But you *did* surpass your father in your business career," I said.

Gerald acknowledged this, but said that because of other problems his work success had not been without hardship. There had been trade-offs. He was reluctant to talk about these "other problems." They were undoubtedly part of some troubled aspect of his emotional life, a common trade-off for professional success.

We talked further.

Gerald realized that on that day when he had had a good medical report (his father had died of cancer), when his business had never been so successful, when he realized that his deeply gratifying relationship with Marlene was headed for permanence, there seemed to be no more trade-offs, no more obstacles.

"Until that day," he said, "I felt unsuccessful because my life was never free of obstacles. Having more money than I knew what to do with did not get rid of the obstacles. But that day was totally problem free."

Nirvana.

But then why the disturbing dream? And why was it recurring?

We continued talking. But Gerald kept drawing blanks now.

"I can't hold on to it," he said. "It eludes me. How the hell do I know why I can't climb that damn monument?"

We all stopped our concentration then and went on to coffee and other talk.

Toward the end of the evening I tried again:

"Tell me, how does it feel to have work success *and* love success? And, equally important at our age, good health?"

"Wonderful," Gerald said, "wonderful." And then, seemingly out of nowhere, as if it had no relevance to what we had been talking about all evening, Gerald said, "Yes, it's wonderful. I've finally got it all. But, you know, there is something that still bothers me. Mostly I don't think about it, but it's always there, always sort of hovering.

"I never went to college, you know. I never had a formal education."

Marlene and I exchanged looks.

Gerald's seemingly "obstacle-free" life was not so obstacle-free after all, at least not psychically. In his unconscious he was thinking, Sure, I'm a big business success, a multimillionaire, but if they ever find out (that I don't have an M.B.A.), the jig is up.

Gerald had to stay down on the ground, with his unsuccessful father, on the bicycle. Being on top of the Washington Monument with the President meant playing with the big guys, with the power brokers. And they all are college graduates.

Or so it went in Gerald's unconscious thoughts.

Since the fear of success is rarely manifested in the realm of our awareness, it's not surprising that Gerald had no idea he suffered from it, mild though his case turned out to be. From all outward appearances, Gerald was totally at ease with his success. Only in his dream life, where he could not control the content with his usual psychic mechanisms, did the conflict show itself.

#2: THE PSEUDO WASP

Frederick grew up in Chicago in the early years of this century in a family of women. His father, an immigrant Polish Jew, had died young in a freak factory accident, leaving his wife Esther, two daughters aged three and four, and Frederick the baby to fend for themselves. The family had been dirt poor when Papa was alive, and with his death they became even poorer. At one point the girls had for beds two kitchen chairs pulled together.

Esther, a moderately bright woman but untrained and unable to speak English, found factory work during the day and at night she cleaned restaurants. During these early days of her widowhood the children were looked after by her younger unmarried sister.

Frederick grew up totally pampered by all four women and although the family continued to be poor, the boy of the house was seldom in want of anything. He was the apple of his mother's eye, without doubt the preferred and privileged child. His aunt spoiled him and so did his sisters.

Esther did not remarry. With her sights focused on a college education for her Frederick she budgeted and saved, often at the expense of her daughters, daughters being expendable items in those days. Within a few years Esther was able to open a small neighborhood restaurant of her own. She promptly pulled her daughters out of school and set one up as assistant cook and the other as head waitress.

The restaurant was grueling work, dawn to dusk, and it never really prospered. However, it did make some money, the better part of which was put into the bank for Frederick's education. He had, by now, decided to become a doctor.

And so, eventually, Frederick went to medical school, often doing his studies at a back table of the restaurant. His mother, always exhausted, and usually smelling of grease, never tired of watching him. She hadn't noticed that her son had become somewhat aloof in his manner toward his family during these medical school days. His sister Ida, who still worked in the restaurant, was the first to notice. She felt hurt and ignored. Ruth, his other sister, had married and was busy having children. She rarely saw her brother Frederick and when she did he spoke to her very little. This was fine with Ruth; she had a new life to see to. It was not so fine for Ida, who was stuck in the restaurant, and stuck with Mama, who by now was not in the best of health. Mama, for her part, noticed nothing detached about her son, even though it was there for the seeing.

When it came time for Frederick's medical residency he was barely speaking to Mama and Ida. He wanted to do his residency in orthopedics and, this being the 1920s, he was convinced his being Jewish would deny him the residency he wanted. Mama, who still had trouble with the English language, Ida, a younger version of Mama, and their tiny ghetto restaurant that was still not prospering served all too well to remind Frederick that he was indeed the son of poor Polish Jewish immigrants. His paranoia mounted to such a pitch that he ended up legally changing his last name to one that he thought sounded "distinguished."

For the rest of his life, Frederick lived in constant fear of exposure.

As a pseudo WASP, Frederick did get the residency of his choice and he did go on to become a very successful orthopedic surgeon. When he married, he married an Episcopalian socialite.

From the day he started his residency, Frederick had nothing more to do with Mama and Ida. He told them to contact him only in case of emergency, and then only as if they were patients, not family; they were to set up an appointment with his nurse/secretary.

Mama, well acquainted with oppression, at first accepted Frederick's wishes; to get ahead, she rationalized, he had to do what he was doing. Later, however, she became bewildered and then finally shamed. She took to her bed and within a year she was dead. Frederick came to the funeral wearing a hat that almost covered his face; he sat in the back and left before the service was over.

Ten years later, Ida fell seriously ill. Her brother-in-law Harold, Ruth's husband, full of anger, called Frederick. Frederick said yes, he would look in on Ida at the hospital but only if she looked upon him as a consulting physician and not as her brother. Harold swore. Frederick held firm; his paranoia had hardened to such a degree that he was able to disregard completely the fact that underneath his refined and sophisticated veneer he bore a striking physical resemblance to his sister Ida.

When Ida died, Frederick happened to be in the hospital tending to one of his patients. He did not go to Ida's room. The next morning Frederick could barely get out of bed; his back had gone out. He continued working, but his back got worse and he was hospitalized. When he recovered, he got in touch with his sister Ruth and asked her to come to his office.

During their visit, it was clear to Ruth that this alien brother of hers wanted some sort of solace and was trying unsuccessfully to reach out to her. He told Ruth he was still ill, unable to keep long doctor's hours, and what was worse, his ailing back curtailed the number of operations he could perform. He also told her he was on the verge of bankruptcy. Not only was his income now cut almost in half because of his illness, but his childless marriage had ended in divorce and the alimony payments were draining him. All in all, he told her, he was quite miserable. And what bothered him most, he said, was that he had no money to give Ruth's children for their education. It did not seem to concern him that he knew neither the ages nor the sexes of Ruth's brood.

Ruth had waited patiently during this interview with her brother for some mention of Mama or Ida. None came. Three weeks later Frederick was found on the floor of his office consulting room, dead by his own hand.

His obituary in one of the dailies began, "Society

doctor Frederick Almond Chase III, born Samuel Rabinowitz . . ."

His secret was finally out.

Many of us try to disguise our identity—or parts of our identity—in some way, a little white lie here, one there, but few of us do so as dramatically as Frederick. Although we cannot neglect the reality factor of how difficult it was for someone who was Jewish to become a doctor (or indeed many other things) in the 1920s, there were others in Frederick's medical school class who did not disguise their Jewish names. Granted, these young men did not become wealthy society doctors in those days, nor did they marry Episcopalian socialites. But they did practice their profession. And I would venture to say that their sense of internal success far surpassed Frederick's—if he had any such sense at all.

There very definitely was a cultural double message operating in Frederick's day: yes, of course this is the land of equal opportunity for *all*, except of course . . . Jews, the Irish, Italians, women, and certainly blacks, among others. Today we tend to forget the hideous discrimination with which many of our non-WASP parents, or certainly grandparents, lived.

The fear of exposure because of a sense of fraudulence is a stellar sign of the fear of success. Frederick's trade-off for excellent career success was that he lived in constant fear of exposure. What this cost him in his personal life, especially during those three-o'clock-in-the-morning times when all of us are alone with ourselves, naked, without masks, can only be imagined. Certainly

Frederick's back trouble was a reality cost. Remember, he was an orthopedic surgeon; his bad back destroyed his practice, thus effectively destroying him; his practice was built at the expense of his mother and his sister Ida—indeed, it could be said that Frederick's practice was built on their backs.

It's not shocking that Frederick's guilt led him to suicide. Guilt of this magnitude has to go somewhere.

7 /

Family Olympics IV

ROLES: BRANDED PINK AND BLUE AT BIRTH

WHERE WE STOOD as children in the psychic constellation of our family and what sort of aura that placement afforded are important factors to be considered in our fear-of-success investigations. As in the cliché Irish family, where one son is designated to be a priest, another a cop, and a daughter to stay home and look after the old folks, each of us had a specific role to play in our family drama. Some of us had major parts, some secondary roles, and some cameo appearances. Others of us were designated to wait in the wings. The equilibrium of the family drama demanded that we stay in our roles. Upstaging a major player would certainly have brought reprisal.

Children play the parts assigned to them to please their parents. The problem child, the preferred child, the inept child, the goody-two-shoes child, the dumb one, the self-sacrificing one, the sick one, the smart one, the healthy one, the precocious one, the scapegoat, the court jester, the runt of the litter—all stay in their roles. As children, we want to please our parents so badly we'd do anything for them, including fail if they want us to.

In adult life we repeat the role assigned to us in our families or we rebel against it. If we should move out of our prescribed roles, we run into trouble. If we rebel against our parents' programing, there are psychic dues to pay. The taking on of a new role is risky and fraught with guilt-inducing possibilities. Most of us do not have an emotional bank balance that permits the option of changing roles. To go, for example, from the quiet one to the grandly assertive is a psychic leap we can integrate only by understanding why we were programmed to be quiet in the first place.

Lucia, a middle-class young woman, had an emotionally disturbed brother and sister who were hospitalized for drug overdoses and she, almost by default, was designated by her family to be the good and healthy one (the one of three who would give her parents no heartache). Thus cast, Lucia received very little concerned care from her parents, who were overburdened with the needs of her siblings.

Lucia felt that she was less interesting than her brother and sister. She says, "I half believed that there was something romantic about craziness, that tortured souls knew the real truth. I always felt that I was not entitled to display the least flakiness since my parents were already overwhelmed by the problems of their other children. Thus I felt deprived. I remember being envious and wishing I could be as sick as they were."

Lucia's need for parental attention once prompted her to become hysterical over some minor teenage trauma. Her mother, who coped by expressing her frustrations in humor, gave Lucia two tranquilizers and said jokingly, "Oh my God, there goes the third one."

One summer as an adult, Lucia again tried to step out of her role. She became depressed, staying home from her job and sitting in her apartment doing nothing day after day. At first she got the concern and care from friends that she had never gotten from her parents. But as is typical, the friends soon tired of her inability to snap out of it. She was not playing the vivacious, polite, emotionally healthy role they recognized.

Lucia emerged from her depression, but she was left with a disquieting feeling that her time (mental illness) would come, as it had for her siblings. She feared this feeling and she flirted with it, until she began to understand why she had been cast in her family drama as she had. When she realized that becoming emotionally ill would not, as she surmised, bring her the sort of parental attention she still craved, she was able to begin building a persona more in keeping with real self.

By the same token, Lucia's problem siblings need to examine the family constellation to discover why they were cast as they were. Aside from possible genetic and/or hormonal factors that may account for a difficult child, the state of the psyches of the parents must be taken into consideration. As we have seen in the case of the schoolboys with reading disabilities discussed in Chapter 2, children who see discord between their parents may offer themselves as problems to heal the marriage. The instability of one member of a family may keep the others afloat. And should the unstable member stabilize, the entire family constellation may be thrown out of kilter.

Clinicians who have observed parents and their schizophrenic child-patient have asked why, if the parental influence is so harmful, the other children in the family are not schizophrenic. Changes in the parental and the family situation provide differing contexts in which children grow up. Did, for example, your family go from rags to riches almost overnight? Did they go from riches to rags?

Did your mother come to belittle your father? Did your father come to browbeat or physically abuse your mother? Did your father come to think of himself as a failure? Did one of your parents develop an alcohol or drug problem? Did one or both of them die?

The psychic constellations of families vary enormously. Who, for instance, took the role of spokesperson in your family, i.e., who ruled the roost? Your father? Your mother? An older brother? Sister? Grandma? An uncle? You? And did the equilibrium shift as you were growing up?

Parenting differs for each child. Were you the firstborn of a brood of eight? Were you the last born of this brood? Were you a middle child, an only girl, bracketed by two brothers? Were you an only child? Was one of your siblings physically handicapped? Was one of them mentally handicapped? Were you physically or mentally handicapped?

If you were a firstborn child in your family, you may have received huge amounts of attention, but you had inexperienced trainers and, perhaps, even anxious ones. New parents who find themselves in the sometimes frightening world of child rearing often seek out child care guidance books. And since there is no one certain path to raising mentally healthy children, new parents understandably get confused and often pass on this sense of confusion to their offspring. For example, a book says it's okay for a child to suck his thumb; no harm will come of it. A new mother is uneasy; she doesn't want her boy to be a thumb sucker. But an expert in a book said it was all right. She lets her son suck his thumb, but her anxiety causes her to pick on him for something else. Perhaps she says, "Go comb your hair, it's a mess," when there is nothing wrong with her son's hair. What she is really reacting to is the thumb sucking. Subconsciously she is thinking, I am letting you suck your thumb, but I don't approve. The son is thinking, There is nothing wrong with my hair; she is being unjust.

By the time this woman's second child comes along, she may have resolved the thumb sucking dilemma—or at least tempered her anxiety about it.

If you are a second child, you may have parents who have less anxiety about raising children, but because there's always that older sibling with whom you must share, you never have exclusive parental attention.

If you are an only child, you may benefit from exclusive parental attention, but that attention may be so overprotecting that it smothers rather than fosters your initiative. Thus independence in adult life may be a problem. And if you are a middle child, you often get ignored.

If you are the youngest child, you may be dismissed as the runt of the litter, always saddled with a feeling of inferiority. Then again, you may be smothered with attention from the grown-ups (which may include siblings) or, in the best of all possible worlds, you may benefit from the mistakes your parents made with the others. Any combination is possible, depending on the context of the family situation when you arrived.

Parenting not only differs for each chronological child, it usually differs radically according to the child's sex. In one of my Family Life–Sex Education classes, a virtually catatonic patient from East Harlem spoke for the first time during a class discussion on the changing roles of men and women. She literally screamed out, "We are branded pink and blue at birth."

Times, as we've seen, are changing, thanks to the efforts of women's move for equity. But social change takes a long time to become integrated into our culture. A recent poll shows that pregnant women, despite the influence of the women's movement, would prefer their newborn to be a boy. The long, sad tale of women's historical oppression has no place in the scope of this book. However, some remarks are in order regarding the fear of success in women as distinguished from the fear of success as it manifests itself regardless of one's gender.

In the early 1960s, a fear of vocational success was thought to be peculiar to men. Women were not seen as having vocations, not "real" women, that is. Real women were home having babies, except for a few flukes and they did not warrant studying. Then, in the aftermath of Matina Horner's now famous 1968 study of women and success, the problem began to be seen as one exclusive to women. My feeling is that a psychological fear of success is a universal fear that may manifest itself in men and women alike, only in women it may take on added virulence because of how society has defined woman's traditional role. In Horner's research, based on 178 University of Michigan undergraduates, she wrote:

A bright woman is caught in a double bind. In testing and other achievement-oriented situations she worries not only about failure, but also about success. If she fails, she is not living up to her own standards of performance; if she succeeds she is not living up to societal expectations about the female role.*

In essence, Horner's study argued that women felt that intellectual achievement and leadership roles, although prized in men, were in conflict with what society deemed appropriate behavior for women. Aggression as we've defined it in the positive sense of to do, to move, to create, to succeed, has largely been frowned upon in women. Passivity, dependency, and incompetence in the world outside the home were the positive female qualities. Social work, once predominantly a woman's field, began to recruit men in 1958 in a declared effort to defeminize the field, i.e., to make it more intellectual, more rational, more scientific, more administrative. It is quite evident that a fear of assertion has fertile soil in which to develop in a woman who assumes the traditional female role.

* Matina S. Horner, "Fail: Bright Women," *Psychology Today*, November 1969.

Today we have women executives and other women holding jobs once not open to them. However, there are few women at the very top of their profession. And even if a woman becomes, say, a vice-president of a large insurance company, it is still basically a token gesture; she usually does not get invited to the informal lunch powwows where her fellow vice-presidents (all male) discuss more business than at any scheduled meeting. She also does not go on their annual brainstorming fishing weekend at some secluded mountain resort. Or if she does go, her anxiety is rampant. And she often gets propositioned by her colleagues, whether she's married or not. It's not all that comfortable for women in the upper reaches of corporate structures. There are usually too many societal and parental negative messages with which a woman executive must deal before she can effectively face the built-in problems of a woman in a man's business world.

Connie was the only woman vice-president in her firm. She was far better qualified than her male peers, thus joining the long list of women who have had to be better than their male counterparts to get the job in the first place. She was aware that her ideas were sound, but she was impatient with the red tape that interfered with the propagation of them. In her judgment, her colleagues conferred an idea to death. She met resistance at every level. She became infected with their uncertainty and began to doubt her own judgment. Presently she developed performance anxiety.

"I no longer can present an idea. I am paralyzed," she said.

The underlying dynamic of Connie's fear is: I am a fraud. If I present myself, I will be exposed. In Connie's case, the societal- and parental-induced sense of fraudulence is: I am a woman in a man's world. I was cast for motherhood. Instead of giving birth to ideas, I should be giving birth to children. My brother was assigned the role of idea man; he was the star of the family. If I succeed, I will surpass my brother, enrage my father, and disappoint my mother. Connie is paying for her business success with constant bouts of migraine headaches and self-doubt.

When she came to understand the casting in her family, she moved on from the role of passive girl child to that of active adult. Parental approval is not a prerequisite for survival as an adult. As an adult, Connie could be an executive, or anything else she chose. She did not have to be a wife and mother, the choice of her parents and of her society.

Everyone says that Carolyn, who is sixty, is the most generous person they have ever met. She is the sort of woman who, when you bring her a bottle of good wine, pulls out a more expensive brand of champagne to toast you. When a friend goes to the hospital, she becomes a full-time volunteer who does the floral arrangements and if the room is grim she will redecorate it. She has been known to cater her friends' weddings and funerals at her own expense.

Carolyn rarely spends money on herself. She wears secondhand designer clothes that she finds in thrift shops and they are usually too small for her. She cooks gourmet food for her friends and then eats the leftovers for the rest of the week. Carolyn is generous, but even her most loyal friends designate her as generous to a fault.

In Carolyn's Family Olympics she had to compete with three brothers who had a better track record than she did. They were being groomed by their parental trainers to be champions. Carolyn was being trained for domestic service. This was not an unusual message for women growing up in the twenties. But for Carolyn it became a constant reminder that she was not as worthwhile as her brothers and therefore she was inconsequential. Her brothers would bring home trophies.

Carolyn bought the family propaganda. She went out and got married as directed at age nineteen. She married a struggling student who was gearing himself to become a certified public accountant. It didn't seem like a noble profession to Carolyn but it became a lifesaver for her. Jack, her husband, was able to earn large sums of money to enable Carolyn to become a hostess with a salon.

Being of no consequence made Carolyn uncomfortable with herself; solitude was to be shunned at any cost. She began to invest in friendships. She purchased friends as diligently as most of us buy our weekly staples. Cultivating people of prominence became a full-time occupation. Her fame, she believed, derived from close association with others who had it. As time went by, she became more discriminating in her acquisitions. A balanced dinner party in her home meant diversification. She invited three actors, two writers, one clergyman, one UN delegate, two artists, and four entrepreneurs. Money did not make you ineligible, but neither did it necessarily get you the best seat at her table. The more successful the friend, the greater was Carolyn's sense of achievement. However, when she won their acceptance, she resented their accomplishments.

Carolyn, like her mother before her, is plagued by negative self-appraisal. Her mother assigned her to an inferior role for having been born female. Mother felt that Carolyn's birth was a sign of her own inadequacy and she transmitted this to her daughter. Carolyn's fight for recognition is not founded on her own strengths and creativity, but on her association with others who have made it. Hers is a loser's battle, since she inevitably experiences herself as less than others. Carolyn's generosity is at her own expense. Indeed, branded pink and blue at birth.

Ben's role in his family scenario was that of being inept, of being unable to do anything right. When he was six years old he was selected by his teacher to be in a Christmas pageant. His father came to see the performance and, within earshot of his son, whispered to the teacher, "I hope Ben doesn't mess up your play."

As an adult, Ben became an actor who found it difficult not to mess up the play. He had a pattern of sabotaging success by causing turmoil in the theater. He complained loudly and abusively saying that the director was incompetent, the playwright mediocre, or the other actors not up to par. They were all inept, he shouted.

Invariably, Ben's belligerent attitude led to his being fired or, humiliated by someone who attacked back, he quit. Methodically he turned every chance into defeat. His reputation soon made it impossible to get work. The word was out: he's a talent but he can't take direction. There were many other talented actors around who could take direction; there was no need to put up with Ben's hostility. He became dispensable.

Ben's father's message to his son was, "Why can't you ever do anything right?"

Ben says, "I think my father thought that putting me down was the right way to bring me up. I can't remember even one reassuring comment from him. However, I can recite a list of knockdown comments that flit through my head almost daily. One of his beauties when I told him I had made the high school football team was, 'What girls' school do you play next?' When I got good grades, he said I cheated. When I got bad grades, he said, 'I'm not surprised.' His opinion of me became a self-fulfilling prophecy. I am a fuck-up."

With time, Ben came to recognize that he had been transferring the rancor that he felt for his belittling father to every authority figure he encountered. Every director, older actor, even playwright became Dad, and in an effort to demonstrate his manhood to them he denigrated them as he had been denigrated. When Ben fully understood the implications of his family programming he accepted the responsibility for having wrecked his career and he decided to try and make a comeback.

He felt uneasy that he would be unwelcome because of his former crimes. His agent had to be convinced that he had changed significantly before he would handle him again. His first endeavor was a workshop production without pay, but with an opportunity to try out his new unbelligerent self. Slowly he rebuilt his career. His first time out in a leading role netted him almost universal praise; there was one bad review. His father called him and referred to the bad review. He said, "Have you thought of being an accountant?" Ben, having pretty much dealt with his anger for his father, replied, "No, but I would love to be an orphan."

Steven had the caretaker role in his family. His job was to compensate his mother as best he could for his father's physical abuse of her. In turn, Steven's mother cared for her son to the point of overindulgence. Theirs was a closely knit, symbiotic relationship.

Until a few years ago, Steven, who is forty-five, and his wife Elizabeth had what everyone considered a wonderful marriage, one that came as near to perfection as could such an imperfect institution. What no one could see, and what they themselves could not see, was that their relationship was composed of a self-destructive sort of love.

Steven and Elizabeth met in music school when both were young singers on the way up. Some years later, at the point where both were doing very well, Steven became anxious about their close relationship. He felt it would suffer if his career shot ahead of his wife's. This fear of sucess led him to give up singing to become his wife's manager. In this way, they could still be together, but they didn't have to compete with each other. In time, Elizabeth became a star. Steven became addicted to pills.

Steven's resentment for having submerged his talent, even though he consciously did it to solidify his marriage, buried itself in barbiturates. Ultimately the drug abuse became so bad he had to be hospitalized. When he emerged, he entered therapy and, in time, he decided to attempt a new career, something that had nothing to do with the world of music.

Consciously, both Steven and Elizabeth felt this step to be essential for Steven's well-being. Unconsciously, they couldn't cope with the separation their now different careers entailed. Elizabeth went into a slump; her career suffered; she became depressed; she missed the loss of constant contact she had had when Steven was her manager. And Steven became depressed because of his lingering need to be tied closely to Elizabeth. They both knew that if Steven continued to pursue his new career, it was inevitable that he would be moving even farther away from Elizabeth. Both of them became somewhat paralyzed by this possibility.

The problem was that Steven had married his mother and Elizabeth had married her mother. They had fused a womblike, safe, secure, relationship based on a neurotic need for affection rather than one based on choice. Steven became Elizabeth's caretaker, as he had been his mother's, and Elizabeth in turn took care of Steven. It became more important for them to be together, to take care of each other, than to be functioning individuals who come together out of free choice rather than out of desperate need. In this particular symbiotic relationship, since both partners suffered from the same needs, it just as easily could have been Elizabeth who sacrificed her career for Steven's. Steven's psyche simply got to that point before Elizabeth's did.

Steven now fully realizes that for too many years

he was more enslaved than enhanced by love. Elizabeth has not reached that point quite yet, although she has consented to enter counseling with Steven. It is to be seen if they will be able to find new pathways for their relationship. My guess, since they are both very receptive to understanding their situation, is that they will be able to tolerate separation and closeness. Only if they insist upon clinging to their childhood roles and to the familiarity of their neurotic need for affection will they not succeed.

I Don't Deserve It Because

BIRTHDAYS AND NAMES

Hotter{H}OW WE FEEL about our birthdays, a good index to our self-concept, is often a result of what we were told about our actual birth. Here are what some parents told their offspring:

- We wanted a boy.
- Such a difficult delivery. I don't want to talk about it.
- You were a mistake, an accident.
- I went blind for a week after your birth; no one knows why.
- Dad got drunk one night.
- You wrecked your mother's womb, no two ways about it.
- I never got my figure back.
- You would not believe the postpartum depression.

With guilt-producers like these kicking around in

one's psyche, who would want to celebrate oneself?

The following is a transcription of a tape I made during one of my Family Life–Sex Education classes with schizophrenics. It was a class in which we started out talking about sibling rivalry but, as in all these classes, the interaction soon took on a direction of its own. In this case, the subject became birthdays.

BETTY: I have an older brother. During the first few years of our lives he did things like stick raisins in my ears and gum in my hair. As we grew older, we grew closer, especially in our teens; we're only three years apart. Our parents were very self-involved and didn't have much time for us. Even though my brother and I were close, there was still sibling rivalry because he was the favorite.
FRIEDMAN: Why was he the favorite?
BETTY: Because he was brighter than I was.
FRIEDMAN: Wait a minute . . . I think there's another reason.
BETTY: No.
FRIEDMAN: You're very bright, so I'm not accepting . . .
BETTY: But they didn't think so, Martha. They thought I was stupid.
FRIEDMAN: But you're not stupid. Could it be that in your family a boy was considered smarter than a girl . . . even if he wasn't?
BETTY: I wanted a chemistry set and I was told that girls didn't play with chemistry sets. Only boys did.
FRIEDMAN: The belief that one has to groom boys to be professional . . .
BETTY: My brother got into a good high school and

then a good college. He was going to be a doctor and I was going to be a teacher.

FRIEDMAN: That's the way your parents programmed it?

BETTY: Which I resented. I wanted to go to journalism school.

FRIEDMAN: So you followed your parents' wishes and became a teacher?

BETTY: I ended up being more independent than my brother. He's a Babbitt. He married young, he works as a stockbroker, he has a home in the suburbs, he has three kids, he plays tennis, he watches TV.

FRIEDMAN: And you?

BETTY: I rebelled. I was a beatnik in college. I lived in black for four years, especially on my birthday.

FRIEDMAN: What does that mean?

BETTY: On my birthday, I made sure I was dressed in black. Well . . . I entered college at sixteen . . .

LAURA: See how stupid you were!

BETTY: . . . and a week later I was seventeen and no one knew it.

FRIEDMAN: I'd like you to explain why you wore black on your birthday.

BETTY: That's what I'm doing. I didn't receive a birthday card from anyone; it wasn't until five in the afternoon that I realized it was my birthday. Ever since, I've been wearing black on my birthday. I'm thirty-four now, and I feel younger than I felt at twenty.

FRIEDMAN: Good.

LAURA: You don't look thirty-four.

JIM: I thought you were twenty-four, twenty-five.

BETTY: I've been married for nine years.

FRIEDMAN: I like what you said, about beginning to

feel young on your birthdays. What do you wear on your birthday now?

BETTY: I still wear black.

(groans from class and from me)

FRIEDMAN: (addressing class) What does this mean, Betty's wearing of black on her birthday?

LAURA: She's in mourning.

MILLIE: Her birthday to her is negative.

FRIEDMAN: She's in mourning for herself?

JIM: She feels she shouldn't have been born.

FRIEDMAN: Betty, you yourself select the black. What does it mean to you?

BETTY: I think it's a day of mourning. A day of death.

LAURA: But in reality it's a day of life, of birth . . . . But I know what you mean; I can relate to that; the worst day of my life was the day I was born.

BETTY: Maybe it's all just superstition.

FRIEDMAN: Why superstition?

BETTY: When I was eleven, things happened to me. I was raped by a man who was forty-five, and that same year when the school I.Q.s came out mine was the lowest. I was teased very cruelly.

FRIEDMAN: I don't see the connection. Would you like to make the connection for me?

BETTY: What happened was that I got very involved with superstition, with the occult . . . horoscopes and . . .

FRIEDMAN: To keep the evil eye off of you? To insure that no more terrible things would happen to you?

BETTY: I'm over all that now. But, you know, the last time I was hospitalized, I was doing devil worship.

MILLIE: You better stay away from that shit.

FRIEDMAN: I'd like to know something. Here you are,

with all this information, with all this understanding of the dynamics of your action, yet you still wear black on your birthday. Can you tell me why?

LAURA: Because she agrees with it.

BETTY: It's not a happy time for me.

FRIEDMAN: You're still mourning your birth?

JIM: She's just stubborn.

MILLIE: Betty, you said before that no one sent you a card? Well, no one will until you recognize your own birthday. About five years ago I started a campaign announcing to everyone that my birthday was coming up. When I was a kid I always got a present or two several days after my birthday; sometimes we'd have a birthday cake, but just with dinner, nothing special. Nobody ever made my birthday special. Not until I started to.

BETTY: You know what happened to me last year? My brother and his family were at my mother's and on my birthday I told them I would bring a cake over and we could celebrate. You know what my mother said? "Don't bother," she said, "everyone's on a diet."

MILLIE: Well, fuck them.

FRIEDMAN: If it had been *my* birthday, I would have bought a cake anyway so that my son would see me celebrating life, not death.

LAURA: Can I say something? I agree with Betty. I do a lot of negative things in my life and I know why I do them, but it's reality. If I said my father beat me because I deserved it, I would be a hypocrite. I have to have a negative attitude.

FRIEDMAN: You wouldn't be a hypocrite; you'd be crazy.

LAURA: Betty *knows* why she wears black on her birthday and she agrees with it. I can relate to that.

FRIEDMAN: Laura, you're saying that there's no room for change. What I want to say is, that's bullshit!

LAURA: I'm talking to you about major trauma!

FRIEDMAN: Major trauma! Who is that, a general in the army? Major Trauma? That's a new one. In the U.S. Army . . . Major Trauma . . . how do you do?

HORTENSE: (who hasn't spoken before) Fuck you all. When it's my birthday, I'll do what I want to do.

FRIEDMAN: Back to you, Betty. One of the things we're taught in psychology is that the first five years are the most important in our lives. But other things happen to us after age five. Positive things can happen. New people influence our lives. New events occur. And we start to change. And it's very frightening to change. But it's important to risk change. If you stay in black, nothing bad will happen to you because you're already in mourning. You're protected. I'm suggesting that you try wearing a bright color to set a whole new tone of celebration. Maybe we'll give you a birthday party. How about it, class? Should we throw a party for Betty?

BETTY: I'm self-conscious.

FRIEDMAN: Too bad about you. You can join Laura's army of major trauma. What do you want to be, Sergeant Trauma? Colonel? Let's pick a date for the party. When shall we do it?

MILLIE: Soon.

FRIEDMAN: How about next Tuesday, is that soon enough? Are you going to show up, Betty?

JIM: What if she comes in black?

FRIEDMAN: We'll kill her. Then we'll all wear black. How do you feel about this, Betty?

BETTY: Embarrassed.

FRIEDMAN: What's embarrassing? Listen, if anyone wants to give a birthday party for me, please feel free to do so.

LAURA: I think a lot of people have birthday problems.

FRIEDMAN: Let's go around, let's see how many have birthday problems.

(Almost the entire class relates some birthday problem.)

FRIEDMAN: It looks like we're going to have to give many parties.

Later in this same class, Laura, who had earlier said that the worst day of her life was the day she was born, took center stage.

LAURA: I think I was a little bit misunderstood on major trauma. It was funny and everything, but I'd like to explain. My mother's birthday is in January. I have never been able to buy her a happy birthday card. Now I know that next Sunday is Mother's Day. My mother keeps throwing hints—Becky is getting me this, Lionel is getting me that. I'm not only not getting her anything, I'm not even going to send her a card. But . . . but . . . I want to. I'm putting myself into such a state. I really must get her something. She's an old woman now. But I cannot wish her a happy birthday. I cannot wish her a happy Mother's Day. It's a trauma. I cannot do it and I want to do it. I want a relationship with her. But I cannot do it. I call that major trauma.

BETTY: Maybe you don't think she deserves it.

LAURA: Of course I don't think she deserves it. But I am stumped by myself. Maybe I should be a little hypocritical. People are hypocritical all over the world. Every day in every way people send cards to people they hate.

FRIEDMAN: Who sends cards to people they hate?

MILLIE: I used to go to the store and look for cards that didn't say anything because I thought my mother was a lousy mother and I didn't want to send one that said, You're the greatest Mom. I never could find any cards that said what a rotten mother someone was. So I picked out the most flowery card with a long verse about how great a mother she was and I sent it. I thought she'd eat it up, and she did. She really thought she was the greatest mom.

LAURA: I hurt my mother tremendously by not sending her a birthday card. I don't want to give anybody the hurt she gave me, not even her.

HORTENSE: That's not true. You'd love to give her the hurt.

LAURA: I can't send my own mother a happy Mother's Day card. That's what I call major trauma.

FRIEDMAN: Here, Laura, listen. I'm going to put your mother in this chair. Is that all right with you? Good. Now tell your mother you're not going to send her a card.

LAURA: (in a trembling voice) I can't send you anything in recognition of yourself as a mother; maybe as a person I feel sorry for you; as a mother I detest you.

FRIEDMAN: Now go sit in the chair and be your mother and answer yourself.

LAURA: (her voice no longer trembling) Don't be silly.

You're so stupid. You know I'm wonderful; all the doctors tell you I'm a great mother. Why don't you listen to them; they know what they're talking about. You're so stupid, you don't even know how good I am, do you?

FRIEDMAN: I'll take over now. Now, Laura, I'm your mother. I'm a grand mother; everybody always says I'm a good mother. I'm going to get cards from the others, and gifts. Now what are you going to give me for Mother's Day?

LAURA: Nothing.

FRIEDMAN: After all I've done for you, you're going to give me nothing? What kind of a daughter are you?

LAURA: Lousy.

BETTY: She just regressed to five years old; she sounds like a little girl.

HORTENSE: You wouldn't believe the way her mother is.

FRIEDMAN: I'm doing the best I can. Okay. Laura . . . are you coming over Sunday?

LAURA: I really don't want to. . .

FRIEDMAN: What do you mean you don't want to? It's Mother's Day. Aren't you going to come over and . . . have a drink with me? (There is a long silence.) I can't hear you, Laura.

LAURA: I'm going to say it, I'm just going to say it. I can never be a mother. And you have been a mother and you have done a lousy job. So maybe it's good I don't have children.

FRIEDMAN: It's not my fault you don't have children. It's not all that great having children. I almost died when you were born.

LAURA: In any event, I cannot wish you a happy Mother's Day.

FRIEDMAN: Why not?

LAURA: Because I don't wish you a happy Mother's Day. I wish you the worst Mother's Day in the world.

FRIEDMAN: I don't really believe you, you know that. I don't believe you for one minute.

LAURA: You're saying I'm stupid. Is that what you're saying?

FRIEDMAN: No, I'm not saying you're stupid. I just don't believe you. . . .

LAURA: Don't you realize you're calling me a liar?

FRIEDMAN: You want to put words into my mouth . . . .

LAURA: You're saying you don't believe me . . . what *are* you saying?

FRIEDMAN: I'm saying that you love me. You couldn't get along without me. And you know it.

LAURA: That's because you breathe for me. I tried to be independent, I tried.

FRIEDMAN: I breathe for you. That's because I'm such a good mother. That proves it.

LAURA: Get away.

FRIEDMAN: You need me too much. I can't get away.

LAURA: You need me too much. I can't get away.

FRIEDMAN: So then we need one another, okay? (addressing class) You can all enter this now.

LAURA: I don't want to do this anymore.

MILLIE: It's too upsetting for her.

FRIEDMAN: It's too upsetting for her? I don't mind upsetting Laura. If this is major trauma, we're sure as hell going to work on it.

HORTENSE: I don't like to see her upset.

FRIEDMAN: You don't like to see her upset? I want her to get through this now.

LAURA: I haven't taken any medicine since yesterday morning.

FRIEDMAN: You can take medicine *after* the class.

LAURA: I don't have any; I have to get some.

BETTY: Don't cop out now, Laura.

HORTENSE: I don't like to see anyone get upset.

BETTY: But she's working it out.

LAURA: Do you mean that if I go through this I'll be able to send that woman a Mother's Day card? Is that what working it out means?

FRIEDMAN: I don't know. I didn't say you should send her a Mother's Day card.

BETTY: But maybe you'll be able to do other things. Like get your own apartment.

LAURA: I already live by myself.

HORTENSE: But you're always at your mother's house. Whenever I try to call you, you're at your mother's. And you know what she does to you. You know what harm she does to you.

LAURA: No, she's getting better.

HORTENSE: She is not. She still puts you down for everything you do.

LAURA: I don't do anything, so I don't give her the chance to put me down.

BETTY: Doesn't she complain all the time?

LAURA: Yes.

BETTY: That's putting you down, complaining.

LAURA: My brother's attitude about me is the same as my mother's.

FRIEDMAN: What is that?

LAURA: He puts me down; he says I'm stupid.

FRIEDMAN: You know, Laura, I find this very interesting. Today on two occasions this class has said how sharp you've been, how helpful. At the beginning, when you said the first child has inexperienced parents . . .

BETTY: It means a lot to the class.

FRIEDMAN: Do you hear this, Laura?

LAURA: It's always easier to help other people.

FRIEDMAN: Oh, I don't deserve to be helped; I don't love my mother, so I don't deserve to be helped. I am not a good daughter, right?

MILLIE: You know, Laura, I like you better when you're working on your problem than I do when you're being so sharp.

LAURA: (agitated) This is turning into a thing.

FRIEDMAN: What does that mean?

BETTY: You're getting it out.

LAURA: You cry, you . . . it doesn't change a thing.

FRIEDMAN: Oh, it doesn't change a thing, eh? Not unless you want it to change.

BETTY: How do you want to feel about your mother?

LAURA: The reason I believe my mother . . . is that I believe I am as she says—stupid—and I try to hide it. You never see me like this. I never allow myself to be seen like this.

BETTY/MILLIE/FRIEDMAN: Like what??

LAURA: When I can't handle anything. When I'm stupid, and I'm dumb, and I'm ignorant . . .

FRIEDMAN: Go ahead, attack yourself some more.

LAURA: I feel so ignorant now, now that I'm letting myself . . . cry.

FRIEDMAN: Oh, showing feelings! It's dumb to show feelings!

MILLIE: Laura, you know you don't look ignorant to

me now. You look more real. Like a person who has some trouble. That doesn't make you stupid.

LAURA: Betty felt so embarrassed about having a birthday party, and that's a happy affair. How do you think I feel, making a scene?

FRIEDMAN: What's a scene? Don't forget, Laura, I set it up.

BETTY: I was crying too and I felt self-conscious for crying.

FRIEDMAN: You too? Why do you feel self-conscious? You get rewarded here for crying.

HORTENSE: You know, all that stuff they feed you . . . talk it out, it'll be fine, just role play, just talk it out. Then take these pills . . .

FRIEDMAN: Pills don't do it all. You *have* to talk! I didn't know Laura felt stupid for crying. If she hadn't talked I'd still not know. Crying means she's getting in touch with feelings. . . .

LAURA: But they're such hurting feelings. . . .

FRIEDMAN: I know. . . .

BETTY: But you suffer anyway.

FRIEDMAN: That's right. There's no psychic rug to sweep them under.

LAURA: Well, I do very well. I've done a lot of sweeping. . . .

What we're talking about here is low self-esteem and guilt. Do you feel worthy of success? Or do you feel, like Laura and Betty, that you're too guilty to be included among the winners?

Laura and Betty, though intelligent, like many people who fall over the edge into schizophrenia, are emotionally disabled. But their lack of self-esteem and their tremendous guilt that leads them to believe they don't deserve success is only different in degree from the lack in those of us who have a mild fear of success.

I often give my students the following sentence completion exercise: "I don't deserve success because . . ."

Here are some of their answers:

Because I lied on my résumé to get the job.

Because I sent my parents to an early grave [they are still alive].

Because it's all been easy for me; it's been tough for my sister.

Because my parents didn't have it.

Because my parents didn't okay it.

Because I split up my parents; it was because of me that they divorced.

Because I cost my parents too much in money and time.

Because my father made it big; I couldn't compete with him.

Because I upstaged my mother in the family drama.

Because I had it so good as the apple of my mother's eye. I'm paying for it in the Big Apple.

Because I am too competitive.

Because I was a bad boy, certainly not as good as my brother.

Because my mother always wrote my school papers.

Because my husband is not successful.

Because my children are not successful.

Because it would take me away from my family.

Because I connived to get where I am; I didn't do it with dignity.

Because I'm all hustle, no substance; I'm doing it with craft, wit, and style.

Because it feels sexually threatening.

Because I got it through seduction.

Because I'm lazy; I only function on one cylinder; I can't handle responsibility.

Because other people deserve it more than I do.

Because I really don't know what the hell I'm doing.

Because I stay in the wings, preparing for the curtain to come down; preparing the tragedy for myself.

Because I haven't done a bloody thing to help myself. My father died and left it all to me. I did nothing to get it. My success came out of tragedy.

Because it's frightening and I don't know why.

Because I wouldn't take care of it, whatever it is.

* * *

Now it's your turn. "I don't deserve it because..."

How we feel about our names is another good index to our level of self-esteem.

It's important what we are called. If we have an ordinary name—Mary, for example—we often feel programmed to be nothing special. We can feel our parents didn't care enough to name us something that would stand out in a crowd. On the other hand, if our name is unusual or unpronounceable and we're made fun of by our peers, it can also be a blow to our self-esteem. A young Spanish patient of mine complained that his mother, having named him Angel, made him think he had to be pure and if he wasn't, he felt guilty. Imagine how a young Jesus may feel. Another patient, whose name is John, said, "You think you got problems? My name is referred to as a toilet."

Nicknames can also be a burden. Being known in the family as Poor Harry or Silly Tillie, or Monkey or Klutzy or Hey, Lazy carries its own problems. And what about those childhood nicknames, dubbings like Fatso, Meathead, Skinny, Dummy? Outwardly such children don't complain much: Call me anything, but let me play with you, i.e., give me affection and approval. However, the internalized toll such nicknames take can be enormous.

Take Fatso. If this is what you were called as a child, you're bound to carry this self-image into adulthood, even if you're now way below what is calculated as a normal weight for your body frame. Maybe you're even very good-looking now, and treated so. No matter; compliments will fall on deaf ears. You'll still perceive of yourself as that ungainly Fat Kid. We carry with us the hurts of childhood. Only if we encourage the Fat Kid within us to express the pain of those early hurts are we able to incorporate a new self-image, that of an adult who is not fat.

Girls with boys' names and boys with girls' names can also suffer. A girl who is named Sydney because her parents wanted a boy can grow up feeling that her real self has been rejected, thus forcing her to sail under false pretenses. What needs working toward in this case is the ability no longer to hear the name as masculine, and the strength to be able eventually to say, "Hey, it's okay to be a woman; my parents may not think so, but that's their problem not mine."

I have found the strongest reaction to what one is called from some men who are named Junior. A man said, "At age forty-five I resent being called Junior. It makes me feel small, like a boy, like I'll never really be a man until my father dies." A younger man felt he could never live up to his father's image, that he would never be grown up enough to be in charge of anything.

I would say that here in very stark terms we can find the Oedipal conflict at work. Boys/men named Junior, no matter their age, often feel like infantilized appendages. They cannot surpass Senior, Daddy, because Junior, Son, usually isn't supposed to do that. So they may feel that they cannot come into their own until Senior dies. And that's a horrifying thought, fraught with guilt.

The problem is not limited to men. I would venture to say that in the movie *Grey Gardens* the Beale women, mother and daughter, were caught in the same bind. While Big Edie (mother) lived, Little Edie (daughter), though well over fifty, had yet to come into her own.

Names *are* important. This was brought home to me during a community meeting I led in a partial hospitalization program for chronic schizophrenics. Even though I was working with seriously disturbed people, the meetings were geared for rationality. I called the patients members and I set down four rules: members had to talk about themselves; they had to try to help others to talk; they could not indulge in off-the-wall behavior (act crazy); and since I was zeroing in on their anger, trying to get them to express it, causing volatile feelings in the air, I insisted that during meetings they could not leave their seats. Nor could they physically touch anyone, even in a positive way. They could scream and yell, "Drop dead!" "I'll kill her!" but they had to remain seated. If they touched anyone, they automatically were kicked out of the program. Everyone had to think rationally and coherently. They had to save their bouts of aberrant behavior for other therapies.

Not knowing these ground rules, a new member, a young man wearing an Indian headband, walked into the meeting one morning. He looked ghastly—pale, disheveled, out of it. He was mumbling. As he walked across the room to an empty seat, I made out snatches of three languages and what sounded like incantations, i.e., this young man had not left his aberrant behavior at the door. When he sat down he continued to mumble and twist around in his seat.

MALE MEMBER: Martha, stop him, he's off-the-wall. Did you hear what he said?

FRIEDMAN: I wonder if we can bring him around to talking rationally.

WOMAN MEMBER: I think he's putting on an act; I wouldn't take him too seriously. I know him from the ward. I was on the same ward.

The young man in the headband turned to the woman and said something rational to her.

WOMAN: I told you it was an act.

FRIEDMAN: Let's see if we can get some more rational statements from him.

WOMAN: I don't want more rational statements from him. Who cares about him? Let him go fuck himself. I didn't like him on the ward, I don't like him now. He's wasting our time.

YOUNG MAN WITH HEADBAND: You fucking nameless whore.

At that, the woman jumped from her seat and started to go for him. She had to pass me; I stepped in front of her.

FRIEDMAN: Get back in your seat. Don't you dare leave your seat! You know the rules.

WOMAN: (breaking down and crying) Did you hear what he said? Did you hear it? He called me nameless.

9 /

Parents Come in Many Varieties

WHAT WERE your parents' guidelines for success? What were they for themselves and what were they for you?

Perhaps your parents never made it and they wanted you to make it. "Be better than I am" may sound like supportive words, both to the parent and to the child, but some children hear the words as a message of low self-esteem, for example, "I'm your parent, but I'm nothing of value," and some parents mean exactly that. This sort of self-deprecation, instead of spurring offspring forward, may indeed become their legacy.

Perhaps your parents never made it and they *didn't* want you to make it. A young man joined Alcoholics Anonymous when he was nineteen. He still lived in the home of his alcoholic parents and was constantly urged to join them for a drink. When he refused, they taunted him: "What's the matter, you too good for us now?" His parents, because of their own unresolved problems, put him in the awful position of having to prove his respect for them by taking a drink, which, for him, would be a self-destructive act.

Of course, not all parents are hostile, demeaning, and destructive. Many are the victims of their own poor parenting and they are emulating the model they learned at home. Again I stress the need for parent education.

Parents come in many varieties. They can be great; or they can be underprotective and overprotective, they can be controlling and belittling and rejecting, they can be too admiring and too seductive. And so on. In the following situations, parents unwittingly programmed their children to avoid success.

Elliot, who is thirty-six, has a work inhibition. It's not that he doesn't want to work (he's had three separate careers already), but that he cannot carry through on any one of his projects. He starts out with great enthusiasm, but when he feels he is on the verge of mastery, his enthusiasm wanes and he moves on to something else. It's not that Elliot is a Renaissance man, exploring and mastering some of the many alternatives life has to offer; Elliot doesn't master anything. He has a pattern of continually starting new projects because he says he gets bored with the old. He justifies his many moves by saying that they show he is versatile. What they really show is that he has a fear of commitment. The boredom he speaks of is a form of depression. Elliot is endlessly in movement because he is avoiding the perils of success.

Elliot first became a lawyer and soon said he got bored with all the details a career in law entails. Then he became a city planner and soon said the bureaucrats with whom he had to work were boring. Then, in a major switch, he opened an art gallery in a summer resort area. At the moment, Elliot is in the process of selling the gallery. He's decided that the resort area is just too boring in the off-season.

As a result of his restlessness, Elliot seldom enjoys the moment, any moment. At a cocktail party he constantly looks over his shoulder, thinking there is something better around the corner. If he's with one woman, he feels he's missing out on someone better. He keeps himself available, his options open. As a result, Elliot receives little gratification from any source. His constant movement from one thing to another serves as an excuse for not having the time to examine his life.

Elliot grew up in a middle-class family in which dependency was encouraged. "I never had to do anything," he says, "and that included practicing the piano, even though I took lessons for five years. I was never given any responsibilities. Once in a while, Mother would trot me out to recite a Joyce Kilmer poem for her guests, but she always stopped me before I finished. I used to have to bow then and leave the room."

Elliot's parents separated when he was twelve years old. Mother gravitated to him as if he were the new replacement for Dad. Elliot had ambivalent feelings about his parents' separation. He enjoyed his new status but simultaneously felt uneasy. He was entering the turbulent stage of adolescence and went back and forth on all issues. Mother reassured him that she would never marry again, which made him both glad and sad. He did not want another man around the house, but he became uneasy about assuming responsibility for Mom.

He saw his father periodically and sensed that Dad thought he was being mollycoddled. Losing Dad's approval made him anxious, so he avoided contact with him; Mother more than made up for Dad's disapproval. She was supportive of him even when she felt he was exploiting her. She rarely said no to him about anything.

After college, in an attempt to gain some independence, Elliot left home and settled in an area a thousand miles away, but his leaving was simply a geographic evasion. Because of his overprotective—i.e., smothering—relationship with his mother, he could not leave home emotionally. Instead of being able to build a successful, independent life for himself, he couldn't help avoiding success by diluting his energies into many different false starts.

When Elliot is between careers, he invariably thinks of returning home. Mother would welcome him back. But he never goes. Instead he takes a new lover who lasts only to the point where there is a chance of real intimacy, then she is banished. Or Elliot seeks out a new therapist, with whom he breaks off as soon as there is the least hint of a beginning of self-awareness.

The manner in which Elliot operates with his careers, switching from one to another, is echoed in his actions with women and with therapists.

Elliot has had a good deal of therapy, but he has never allowed a rapport to develop between him and the therapist, let alone a breakthrough. The therapist always becomes too boring, i.e., too stupid, too poorly trained, too insensitive, and so on.

The first therapist Elliot consulted was a dyed-in-the-wool Freudian who recommended psychoanalysis. After six months, just as he was beginning to understand a little about himslef, Elliot became vocally opposed to Freudian analysis, calling it bullshit.

He next consulted a woman who was a bioenergetic therapist. He felt as infantilized by this therapy as he felt by his parents. A third therapist recommended medication. Elliot was not opposed to medication, but he argued that it was the wrong sort for his particular problem. Next he went to est and left there feeling he was an asshole. In group therapy, where he lasted longest, he never talked about himself but was big on analyzing others.

People who go into therapy to defeat it, like Elliot, have a serious fear of success.

It is too often assumed that the overprotective parent is all-caring. However, we have come to recognize that the opposite may well be true. Overprotection can cover up rancor against the child. In Elliot's case, Mother's need to keep him with her contributed to infantilizing him. Whatever the motivation, the end result is destructive. The overprotected child generally feels incapable of tackling the outside world. He has been thwarted in his endeavors to assert himself. His fears of taking the initiative are reinforced by parental concerns about his every movement.

Andrea is a workaholic and answers to the designation. She's also a Trollope fan and has passed along to me these words from *Orley Farm*: "There is no bliss equal to twelve hours of work with only six hours in which to do it." Andrea has worked in this manner since the age of seventeen. She's forty-three now, and is beginning to be a very wealthy woman. It is time, she feels, to slow down a little, to play a little. But she finds it difficult to relax enough to do so.

Andrea owns and manages a restaurant. It's a seven-day-a-week operation. She has always worked long hours, not only because she is a woman in business for herself, but because time spent away from work makes her uneasy. To Andrea, fun and relaxation are a waste of time. And time is always in short supply. When friends suggest pleasurable activities she usually says, "I have no time." She has a dread of leisure. She has, for instance, never been on a picnic. She never takes a vacation, and she has never spent a day just bopping around doing nothing. She has enough money now to do any of these things, but she is pleasure-inhibited.

Andrea feels best when she has complete control of things, when she believes she is self-sufficient. Only when she feels totally secure and in control does she allow herself a move toward intimacy with someone. Otherwise closeness makes her anxious. As with many workaholics, Andrea is a business success, but she suffers from a fear of emotional success.

Since both of Andrea's parents were alcoholic and indifferent to her needs, she learned early to hold her feelings in, to rely only on herself, to trust only herself. If she needed clean clothes for school, she washed them herself; dinner was often a can of cold corned beef hash. Underprotected by parents who were off in a world of their own, Andrea had too much responsibility too soon and no one on whom to lean, ever. She felt unsafe, became emotionally withdrawn and outwardly strong.

Andrea's workaholism not only serves to bury her anxieties and fears, it has enabled her to amass enough money to feel safe, as she never felt as a child. With money she needs no one; she stockpiles it to feel secure.

Andrea looks positively upon herself as a hard worker and she is that; she is productive, reliable, energetic. She thinks of herself as an independent person, and that's not a bad thing to be. What she doesn't realize is that an overly self-sufficient person is really denying deep dependency needs. Rather than being independent (which a person who does not have a fear of intimacy can also be), Andrea is detached, emotionally unavailable. It takes time to develop intimacy with someone and Andrea has no time. All of her energy goes into her work and there is none left over to share joys, fears, fantasies, worries, experiences with someone. Her work is the protection she never got as a child. It makes her feel safe. The trade-off, as Andrea was aware of enough to verbalize, is, "There's nothing worth opening the champagne for." With that sort of recognition of her life, she has taken the first step toward being emotionally available enough to trust.

How many times have you heard, "If only I had money . . ." Perhaps you've even said it yourself. Who could have a fear of success with money? As we've just seen, Andrea and Elliot could answer that question for you. I have also come across many cases in which inherited money or the expectation of inherited money has fostered a fear of success. For example, Phillip.

Phillip retired from the world of work at thirty upon receiving a large inheritance from his maternal grandfather. He said, as have others, that inherited money is tinged with morbidity. I asked Phillip if perhaps it was not a sign of love that his grandfather had left him the money. "Sure," he replied, "but it enabled me to do nothing and hence I have become nothing."

When he was twelve, Phillip went off to the country with his mother. He wanted to do something with his free time so he applied for a job at the country club; the thought of getting paid for work made him feel adult. He felt the man in charge treated him with respect for his ambition and went out of his way to find something for him to do that would pay him a small salary. His job was to pick up refuse and cigarette butts from the grounds. When he told his mother of his job she was appalled and told him to go immediately and resign. She went on to say, "It's beneath the dignity of my image of you."

Phillip's parents never urged him to work. Ten years after his inheritance, when he was forty, Phillip said, "I have never done anything worthwhile in my life." With that attitude, he did not feel entitled to success. It's not without cause that the phrase Poor Little Rich Boy/Girl has come into being.

Albert, age fifty-four, used to be a perfectionist. He rated everything in life, from movies and restaurants to people, on a scale of one to ten. He had to be surrounded by the best of everything—the most perfect haircut, the restaurant with the most perfect wine cellar, the most perfect school for his son, the most perfect wife. This may seem to be an attempt at excellence but, in actuality, people who are driven by a compulsion to be perfect may be trying to cover up their shortcomings, and thus avoid belittlement. Perfectionists may harbor a feeling of being defective. And, as such, they usually fall far short of the mark they themselves set up. Nothing they ever do is good enough.

Albert makes his living designing textiles. At the time I'm talking of, he had received a good deal of acclaim in his field but, in his mind, the accolades were not justified because he knew how flawed he was. When he was given praise, he denigrated it by saying, "I could have done better; it wasn't my best effort." He was agonized by the fear of making a mistake that would expose his shortcomings. He had a fear of success.

Albert reports growing up in an atmosphere of hostile competition. He was a preferred child; his sister was sickly, requiring more than the normal amount of care. Albert's preferential treatment never gave him a sense of being loved; it seemed more like a demand than a reward for effort. In the family constellation, Albert's sister was designated a disappointment. She was beyond hope; Albert had to compensate. He tried to be an ideal, model child. He did his homework systematically and was consistently rewarded with top marks. He remembers bringing home a paper that not only was marked 100 percent but had a gold star attached to it. His mother (who had a habit of saying, "There is no room for error in this life") asked him who else got a gold star.

His mother talked approvingly about him to others but she never gave him praise directly. Nothing he did was good enough. As a consequence, he felt defective. Neither did Albert's father get approval from his wife; she headed a one-woman faultfinding commission and Albert's father tacitly went along with her ways. As hard as they tried, nothing Albert or his father ever did was good enough for Mother. Father and son always fell far short of the mark.

Early in his teens Albert was recognized as a creative talent. He wanted to be a painter, but felt he could not compete unless he was as good as Picasso. How could Albert compete? He was riddled with flaws his mother had pointed out only too often. He decided on a career in textile design, and became well-known and highly regarded in the field. At the height of his success, he began to suffer from dreadful insomnia.

The head of the firm under whom Albert worked was a man who demanded perfection. He never gave praise directly, but if business was bad, there was hell to pay up and down the company line. Albert came to believe that his boss could see through him, could see his defects. As a result, Albert drove his crew of co-workers to tears in his own demand for perfection. His insomnia got so bad that he found himself lying awake at night, fearing the exposure of what he called his errors. He felt he would go to work the next morning and all would be over; he would have been exposed for the phony he was.

During this period, rival firms gave Albert several enticing job offers. He rejected them all, opting for what he called job security, even though the pressure from his boss was so great he was on the verge of leaving several times. Each time he panicked and each time his boss, having sensed that he was about to leave, gave him a substantial raise. He never gave him praise.

Albert finally realized that he was working for Mama. When he gave way to the rage he felt for his mother's constant belittlement while he was growing up, he simultaneously saw that his disparaging boss was a reincarnation of his mother. His boss was the equivalent of Mama's one-woman faultfinding commission. This discovery enabled Albert to move to another firm and to pick one with a boss who was able to give praise where praise was due. He finally saw that his excuse of job security was a rationalization, an unconscious need to stay in a situation that reenacted the hostile atmosphere that had existed in his Family Olympics. Years of anxiety were lifted the day that Albert, no longer a perfectionist, was able to say to himself, It's all right to make a mistake.

10 /

Death, the Ultimate Fear of Success?

FOR SOME OF US the achievement of a long-desired goal is tantamount to getting the death penalty. In fact, it well may be that the ultimate fear of success is the fear that we will die when a goal is reached. Some people ward off the fear of dying by killing themselves. Some take flight and go into hiding. Others find themselves midway through a project and are unable to finish it.

Andrew, a young man who devoted all of his nonjob hours to the building of boats, once found himself in just such a situation. He was working on a project and thought he would die if he finished it.

Andrew is in his middle thirties, a good-looking man who's a little overweight and doesn't talk much. When he does talk, he has a slight, very slight, stutter. He's the proverbial nice guy, the one in the crowd who always drives everyone home no matter how inconvenient. He never complains. Life happens, he watches. He does little to steer it down one path or another.

No one would ever accuse Andrew of being a dynamo. With his passive stance, there is precious little that Andrew even gets excited about. But there is *one* thing.

And that's the building of boats.

Andrew is an amateur builder of boats. It started with model boats when he was eight years old. Through the years the models became more sophisticated and he chalked up a respectable win-loss record at various rivers and lakes near where he lived. When he was eighteen he began to dream of building a full-scale racing boat, one he himself could navigate; he even fantasized about entering competitions and, step by step, winning all the trophies to be had. In no other area of life was Andrew as accomplished as he was in the building of model boats—a skill that didn't count for much in his family. He, being the oldest son, was destined for college whether he wanted to go or not; the building of a full-scale racing boat remained a fantasy. In fact, he told no one of his dream until many years later when a friend who had inherited a broken-down barn asked Andrew what the hell he could do with all that empty space. To Andrew's complete surprise, and to the surprise of his friend, he found himself summoning up every ounce of assertiveness he possessed and saying, "Let me build a racing boat in it."

I met Andrew at the point where he could not finish building his boat. The friend who had inherited the barn had taken Andrew up on his desire, and for two years, utilizing every moment of spare time, Andrew had been totally absorbed in the construction of his boat. He told me that those two years had been the very best of his life.

To finish the boat all Andrew had to do was apply three coats of varnish. But he could not bring himself to do it. He was paralyzed with an inertia that he could not explain. He developed muscular spasms that were diagnosed as resembling arthritis, and was advised to remain physically inactive. In a way he welcomed the illness because now he felt he had a legitimate excuse to postpone the finishing of his boat.

Why such a block? Why could Andrew not see to completion the one thing in life that meant the most to him?

As I got to know Andrew, it became clear that a fear of success was deeply ingrained in his psychic makeup.

Andrew is the oldest of two children. His father is a businessman, his mother is a professional, and his younger sister is a scientist who already is making a mark in her field. Andrew drives a bakery truck to make a living. He's been doing this for the last ten years.

When he was in elementary school, Andrew had a mild reading disability. A reading disability, whether mild or severe, does not necessarily reflect low or even average intelligence, but it does carry with it the certainty of lowered self-esteem.

Andrew had a perceptual problem, and he had a "progressive" schoolteacher who told him to notify her if he ever got the urge to learn to read. This is a good technique to use when facing the resistance of a child who adamantly refuses to learn, but since Andrew never had refused to learn to read, the teacher's attitude backfired and helped to lay the groundwork for his later resistance to learning.

To get an idea of what the alphabet looks like to beginning readers, try glancing at a shorthand text. When Andrew did open a book, he found the symbols incomprehensible; he informed the teacher that he would not be ready to read for a long time. She accepted his decision. "Don't hurry and don't worry," she said. "All in good time." It sounded reasonable, but it was not exactly therapeutic when some of Andrew's peers finished their primers and were well into first-grade readers.

Andrew couldn't read, but he was the best block builder in the class. When he became annoyed with a precocious peer who was already reading comics of the classics, Andrew would throw one of his blocks. Or sometimes a punch. Whereupon his teacher, bending over backward to be progressive, but merely sounding false, would say, "You must learn to stop yourself, Andy." What she should have done was to teach him to read.

Andrew ultimately developed an inhibition of aggression. It was not primarily the teacher's fault, of course, but her attitude and influence certainly exacerbated his difficulties.

Andrew's parents had been in agreement with his teacher's technique until they realized that their son was making a permanent decision not to learn to read. They decided to hire a psychologically-oriented tutor whose mission it was to break the reading block. The tutor observed Andrew making complicated model boats. He asked him what he did about reading the building instructions.

"My father reads them to me," Andrew replied, more in sadness than in shame. "The trouble with my father," he added, "is that he always wants to make the boats himself. I tell him to buy his own, but he is a grown-up and he just keeps doing mine until I end up crying."

The tutor wisely taught Andrew how to read from a manual on how to build model boats. Learning to read, even prose with difficult technical words, is easy if the words are of value to the reader. Andrew became proficient in reading, but narrowed his selections to boating magazines and books. He went on to college but left after his sophomore year, believing he was reading literature for which he still was not ready. He went to work for his father, who is a building contractor.

It was as an apprentice carpenter that Andrew joined his father's crew. Soon he became more adept than most of the men with whom he worked. His father, who supervised the jobs, rarely trusting that anyone would be as competent as he, observed his son and talked about him with pride—but never complimented him directly. He admired the skill and patience his son had, but he never put him in charge of a job, nor did he make him a foreman; he said he couldn't play favorites. What was really happening was that Andrew was well on the road to surpassing Daddy, and this was psychologically impossible for him and for Dad. Andrew would remain in the category of permanent apprentice as long as he worked for his father's firm.

Having fallen into a pattern of passivity, Andrew continued to work for his father. He even joined the carpenters' union, but after a while he stopped paying the union dues. When his membership was cancelled, his father was furious. This enabled Andrew to leave. Since he was married by this time, and since he and his wife were expecting a child, he took a secure job below his potential. He started driving the bakery truck. He rationalized that it was well worth it not to be in the same field as his father.

And so for a number of years Andrew drove his bakery truck, played with his daughter, and built his model boats. He rarely saw his father. Then came the opportunity from the friend with the barn to build his dream boat, the full-scale craft he could navigate and race himself.

Andrew worked steadily for two years. When the boat was almost completed, he showed it to some of his friends and they were impressed. His father asked to see it, but he wouldn't show it to him. The man who had lent Andrew the barn declared him a master craftsman and himself a patron of the arts! Externally Andrew was no longer an apprentice.

Success at last?

No.

It was shortly after his friend's ultimate compliment, on top of everyone else's admiration, that Andrew lost interest in finishing the boat, in applying those last three coats of varnish. His wife who, during the building of the boat had complained about all the time he spent in the barn, now became concerned about his disenchantment with the project. She encouraged him to finish, but the more she did so the more resistant he became. He began to resent her prodding.

It was at this time that Andrew's father was hospitalized. And in one of those truth-is-stranger-than-fiction coincidences, his father shared a hospital room with a young man who was a victim of a racing boat accident. When Andrew summoned the courage to visit his father in the hospital, the first thing Dad did was to point to the bed next to him where the young man lay immobile.

"Racing boat victim," Father told son. "Smashed up in the water by another racing boat nut."

Andrew's mother repeated the same words. Racing boat victim. And added, "Paralyzed for life." It was the type of warning his parents had long ago agreed to convey to him for his own good. He tolerated their attitude because he knew that his desire to race boats was a source of anxiety for them. What his parents didn't know was that he was scared to death even to finish building his boat, let alone race it. And at this point Andrew didn't know this fact himself.

Although Andrew is squeamish about being in hospitals, while his father was hospitalized he visited him every day—and ended up spending most of the visits talking with his father's roommate, the boating accident victim. Andrew brought along his latest boating magazines and read aloud to the bedridden young man. When the young man, who hadn't yet been told of his permanent paralysis, told Andrew that the hardest part of being laid up was that it prevented him from racing, Andrew encouraged him to return to the water as soon as he was able. The two became good buddies.

Because of his contact with this young man and because of all the boating talk, Andrew had a spurt of interest in his boat. He began to think about putting on the finishing varnish strokes. But he procrastinated. Instead he ended up spending several weekends sanding and waxing his apartment floors.

Two years passed before he touched his boat again.

The breakthrough to understanding for Andrew came after a year of counseling. During a good deal of that time he suffered from nightmares; he would awaken drenched in the perspiration of anxiety with a feeling that he was going to die. Slowly he connected this feeling to the finishing of his boat; if his boat were finished, he would have to race it; and if he did race it, he felt he would have a fatal accident.

To Andrew, finishing his boat meant death.

At first, on the surface, as he sought understanding, it appeared as if his daily viewing of the racing boat victim, immobile, paralyzed, had kept him from finishing his boat. On further delving, it became clear that his own paralysis had set in long before he met the racing boat victim.

Through counseling that included a charting of his Family Olympics, Andrew became aware that his real feeling of terror and death did not have to do with boat racing at all, but with his relationship to his father. If he finished his boat, it didn't mean that he had to race it, but it did mean that he would have moved out of the apprentice carpenter role, into which his father had permanently cast him, and into the role of master craftsman. Because of the enormous guilt Andrew felt about his buried rage at his father for casting him in the permanent role of apprentice and denying him the role of master craftsman, the latter role held terror for him. He felt he would be punished for his rage. He felt he would be killed if he became a master.

Andrew's nightmares about being killed in a racing boat accident were merely the manifestations of feelings he could not face in his conscious thoughts.

With his new understanding, Andrew decided to give up the idea of racing boats. At the same time he stopped his automobile speeding, an addiction that had led to many tickets and the suspension of his license. Since he would never race his boat, he decided to sell it. This decision enabled him to finish the boat, which he did during a two-week vacation from his job. However, when the boat was finished, he found that he could not part with it. He had begun to look upon it as his best piece of sculpture. He sold the boat's motor and kept the boat.

The last time I heard from Andrew, he had left his bakery truck job. With the friend who had lent him the barn and, upon seeing the boat Andrew built, had declared him a master craftsman, he was about to open a business having to do with the restoration of old boats.

Andrew's strategy to avoid punishment for the rage he felt toward his father had been to postpone the varnishing of his boat. He came to believe that he preferred to wax the wooden floors of his apartment. When that ploy no longer worked for him, he caught a mysterious ailment diagnosed as resembling arthritis, and this kept him from working on the project. His psyche could encompass anything, as long as it wasn't success.

Andrew had an inability to do what he really wanted to do, to do it very well, and to feel good about himself doing it. When he was able to discover and deal with the underlying cause of his fear of success, the threat of the death penalty was lifted.

Zoe, a well-known painter, had an experience similar to Andrew's. She told me that she once felt she would die when a certain series of paintings she was working on would be finished. The subject of one of the paintings was a treatment of human suffering in World War II.

Zoe considered this work significant above all her other works, which were considerable and which were represented in major museums. She called this work her masterpiece.

She worked furiously on this series, isolating herself in the country with only her dog for company and painting as if obsessed. One day and night when she was snowed in, she painted for so many hours that when she finished at five in the morning she couldn't lower her arm. For hours she had been standing on a six-foot scaffold with her arm and brush extended to reach the very top of the huge canvas. When she got down from the scaffold she found herself walking around with her arm stiffly in the air; only with massage did the arm return to its normal state.

Zoe was half-convinced she was actually going to die when she finished the painting, even though she consciously dismissed the thought as just too bizarre. She kept on painting, sometimes uneasily, sometimes with frenzy. Then she developed migraine headaches and hypoglycemialike symptoms that slowed her down, sometimes to a standstill.

The only thing that Zoe did, other than work, during this period was to buy herself an elaborate Victorian marble angel that she put in her garden in a spot where she could see it from her studio. She said there was no doubt in her mind that she had bought the angel not only to serve as garden statuary, but eventually to serve as her tombstone. The angel even held a scroll and on that scroll she planned to have her name carved.

Zoe was shocked to realize that she seemed to be preparing for her death, even though she consciously hadn't the least desire to be dead.

In her Family Olympics, Zoe had a number of factors that could lead to a fear of success. For one thing, by becoming a nationally known artist she had broken her family programming. In her traditional family she had been expected to be a full-time wife and mother—nothing more and certainly nothing less. In addition she had far surpassed her brother in career success. Although her brother had been groomed to be the star professional of the family, he had never been able to pull it all together, despite flashes of brilliance. His emotional life was similarly unsuccessful. And Zoe had been extremely close to her father, to the extent of mourning his death for a full year and carrying his name through two marriages (this was some years before it became a feminist statement to maintain one's maiden name).

There were definitely vestiges of Oedipal and sibling

conflicts in Zoe's psyche, but aside from these two classic success inhibitors, Zoe had the additional problem of the subject of her painting.

In her painting she was dealing with human suffering. And the manner in which she was treating it was bound to be controversial. She was thus putting herself in a dangerous situation. Because of the controversial nature of the painting, she was leaving herself wide open for critical attack. She also found herself in the double bind of wanting to depict suffering in her art but at the same time realizing that she would profit from the suffering—that she would be rewarded both professionally and monetarily. The overwhelming guilt thus engendered made the unconscious price for such a masterpiece her life.

Zoe did finish the painting. It caused a stir in the art world and was reviewed favorably except by one critic. In telling me about this negative review, Zoe said, "I was so brutally hurt by this critic it was as if she had wanted to take a hatchet and literally kill me." She then told me that twenty years previous, when she was first showing her work, this same critic had done a similar hatchet job on one of her early shows.

Perhaps this long-ago review, supposedly integrated into this famous artist's psyche, had not been so integrated after all. This situation, too, could have contributed to Zoe's fear that death awaited the completion of her project.

Midway through their projects, Zoe and Andrew developed illnesses that for a time kept them from continuing their work—Zoe the headaches, Andrew the illness resembling arthritis. Another person I know, a writer, temporarily went blind.

About a year ago, Lily called to let me know she had received a huge advance of money for her new book and she was having a terrible anxiety attack. Before I realized she was being serious, I told her that I too had just received a book advance but it was so minuscule that it wasn't even worth getting excited about, much less anxious. She laughed, but then she said she had an ominous feeling she would not live to see her work published.

One way to allay anxiety is to minimize the importance of what is causing the distress. I asked Lily if in her estimation her book was a Pulitzer Prize winner.

"No! Of course not," she said. "It's not that sort of book."

Then I implied that it probably wouldn't even make the best-seller list, so what was she anxious about? At first she seemed to be relieved, but then she became angry. "Why not?" she shouted. "It'll be just as good as some of the others on the list." Then we went on to talk of other things.

I didn't hear from Lily again for several months until a relative of hers called to say she was in the hospital with an eye infection that had caused her to lose her vision. The relative, who was psychologically oriented, said that what was more frightening than the blindness was the fact that Lily was not hysterical with grief, but was taking her illness very calmly, accepting the fact that she was incapacitated.

I went to visit her and indeed saw that she was very complacent, listening quietly to tape recordings of books for the blind. I was struck by the boxes of the tapes on her bedside table. They were the same as those my husband had been using the last months since a debilitating stroke had left him legally blind. Since his teens, my husband had been a great reader; a day that began without the *New York Times* was a rarity. It was a source of anguish to see Lily, also a great reader, in the same predicament. I confided in her; my feelings of grief for both of them reached Lily and she started to cry, but as she did so she became frightened of harming her eyes and reached to cover them. I quickly said, "It can only be therapeutic to cry; don't block the tears."

She cried for a long time. Later that day her doctor saw that the white film that had covered her infected eye seemed to be clearer; after further examination, he told her the infection was healing nicely and he didn't doubt she would be going home in a few days. When he told her this, instead of being ecstatic, Lily complained of more pain.

Lily eventually did go home, with her sight restored. It is clear now that she had wanted to stay in the hospital, she had wanted to remain blind, for in that way she had a legitimate excuse not to continue with her book. Her illness meant she no longer had to risk death by assuming the responsibility for becoming a success—just as Andrew's illness had kept him from working on his boat and Zoe's headaches had kept her from working on her painting.

In Lily's Family Olympics there figured a very beautiful mother, a self-styled Beauty Queen, who wanted Lily and her brother to worship her. To that end she pitted the children against each other, broke up the possibility of closeness between them, and proceeded to dominate them both. Mother needed constant admiration and Lily grew up with a fear of surpassing her. Lily was programmed not to be as successful as Mother.

Lily did live to see her book published; it did not make the best-seller list, but it had a very respectable run. Her anxiety came and went once she got back to working on the book, but she no longer felt she was going to die. In a way she had paid her dues by going blind; to a reader and writer, a loss of vision is surely a sort of death.

11 /

The Kid's a Riot

NOW THAT I'VE related the fear-of-success patterns of so many of my students, patients, friends, and acquaintances, it seems only fair that I should add to this exploration my own dynamics.

Many of us who work in the field of psychology often specialize in a psychological problem we ourselves have. And if we don't actually specialize in it, then at least we give it extra attention. I am no exception. One of the best examples I can give of someone who has had a rampaging fear of success—and has overcome it, not entirely but sufficiently—is myself. Here are all the gory details, including a flagrant example of an unresolved Oedipal conflict along with a debilitating case of sibling rivalry.

My father told me that when I was born, he instructed the doctor "to put it back." He already had a daughter, my sister, born four years before me.

I don't really believe that my father told the doctor to put me back, but that is what he said to me so frequently in my childhood that I spent most of my young years in a bind. I tried to be the son he wanted and the girl I was. Trying to get his approval, I did many foolish things like roller skating down dangerous hills that frightened me.

I also tried to be perfect.

In order to be perfect in our family you had to be outgoing, cheery, and funny, funny being the most important. Anyone who visited our household and told a hard luck story was labeled "a crepe hanger." If you were sad, you were automatically designated a loser. And losers were dead as far as my family were concerned.

I caught on to the system early on. I knew that in order to please my father I had to be hilarious—and good at daring exploits. So I performed. I joked and clowned and roller-skated tough hills—I was Daddy's little girl. "She's such good company," my parents' friends said, "such a good kid," This often made me the center of attention at their bathtub gin parties.

In those early years, I really pleased them, so I was given their highest rating: the kid has a good personality, i.e., she's a riot. To all concerned, I was a smiling, wisecracking five-year-old, approved of by my parents and their friends. It seemed to be an ideal situation in which to grow up. But it was not.

When my parents rated me as having a good personality, it was usually while they were comparing me to my sister, whom they said had *no* personality. That meant that my sister was not funny. She did not have their prescribed sense of humor. She was, as a matter of fact, a shy and withdrawn child. And no wonder, since at the time of which I am writing she was severely handicapped with polio.

My sister had a noticeable limp. At table she could hold a fork and knife but only with difficulty. She was poorly coordinated physically and in many ways paralyzed emotionally. Imagine being in a family whose first priority was laughter and good times, the devil take tomorrow, when you, a victim of polio, had a difficult time walking and eating.*

Young as I was, and even though I loved being Daddy's favorite and knocked myself out to keep his attention, I felt somehow that the competition between my sister and myself for my parents' approval was horribly unfair; I felt this, but I didn't understand it. Nor did I know what to do with it.

When I defeated my sister which, because of her handicap, I always did, I felt less than elated. But I continued to win because my parents, in their immaturity and inexperience (one may end up forgiving parents after understanding them), escalated the competition by praising me and punishing her. I began to believe that I was some sort of bad seed. The whole thing was rigged; all I had to do to win was to perform, put on an act. I wasn't being recognized for being myself. In essence, I was being rewarded for being a fraud.

Winning the sibling competition was all well and

* Today my sister walks without a limp. She recovered completely from that early poliomyelitis. And in keeping with the dictates of our family, she became a great raconteur and is appreciated for her humor.

good at the time. Only in retrospect have I really realized just how incredibly unfair the competition had been. My victory had been at my sister's expense. In classic sibling rivalry fashion, this victory turned out to be one of the most guilt-producing triumphs of my life.

I was very definitely the preferred child. And as we have seen, being the preferred child does not guarantee a successful adult life. In fact, depending on the degree of lingering guilt about siblings, it frequently leads to quite the opposite. In my case, it helped to create a fully flowering fear of success.

As did my other battle. Winning Daddy from sister was easy. But I also won a much more dangerous competition. I won Daddy from Mommy.

My parents never really got along. They married at an extraordinarily young age, my mother at sixteen, my father not much older. Both were escaping. My mother was fleeing a life of drudgery in her mother's business and household. My father wanted a home. His mother had died soon after his birth and for a few years he was raised by his father's new wife—until they sent him to an orphanage. Knowing this story at an early age, I was especially careful to please Daddy so as to help compensate for his painful childhood.

When my parents married, neither of them understood what marriage entailed. In those days nobody talked about marital contracts, hidden agendas, compatible psyches. Open marriage went on behind closed doors. It was sinful. All people were expected to marry, most of them ignorant of the intricate puzzle they were getting into. Nor, when my sister contracted polio, were

my parents in any way prepared to cope with a handicapped child. They resented her physical and emotional
disabilities, looked upon them as a rebuke to themselves.

And they fought. How they fought. My father
wanted an old-fashioned wife. Instead he got a jazz-age
flapper who smoked and wore paint on her face, having
been liberated from her mother's sweatshop in the roar-
ing twenties. In its way, this helped my father to focus
his attention on me. He called my mother an un-
natural mother, accusing her of treating me like an
orphan. The closer my father and I became, the greater
my mother's enmity became—and the more I feared her.

Every Monday my father took me, age five, to New
York's Palace Theatre. My mother and sister never got
to go. Once home, my mother's wrath descended on
my father. And then on me. Because she was young and
unknowing, it was easy for her to hold me responsible
for their troubles. Or at least that's how I read it. I do
recall deftly pitting one against the other and feeling a
measure of guilt about it. My mother loudly accused me
of having taken her husband's love away from her. I
had become a five-year-old femme fatale—instead of the
funny little girl she liked to show off to her friends.

Later my mother became abusive. The physical attacks were less painful than the name-calling. "Trouble-
maker" was the worst. I really felt I *was* the trouble-
maker; I believed that I had instigated the fights which
caused the rift between them. When she said I was no
good, that I would never amount to anything because
I was rotten to the core, I believed her.

Although having Daddy prefer me over Mommy was

nifty, had it been possible to realize the crippling psychological strings with which such winning came, I would rather have lost that particular battle.

There was one aspect of my early family life at which I was not victorious. The experience served to help imprint on me an unhealthy definition of success under which I operated for far too many years.

During the latter part of my childhood, I had an uncle who lived with us while he was an intern at Bellevue Hospital. His mother, my maternal grandmother, while on her deathbed, made her daughter, my mother, promise to see her younger brother through his medical studies, even if it meant that my mother and her family had to do without food.

My mother kept that pledge. When my uncle needed books, we ate potatoes. My father took out a bank loan to help pay my uncle's tuition, and then struggled to meet the payments. To win what was becoming a losing battle, my mother decided to become a bootlegger. At age eight, I had to make the deliveries. I knew that I was involved in an illegal operation which was frightening and degrading at the same time. My mother explained that the end justified the means. My uncle, once a doctor, would command so much respect there would be enough left over for us. My uncle was already the fair-haired member of the neighborhood; street toughs didn't mess with him. We were the only family on the block that had a telephone. We had a doctor in the house! Respect and dignity were already ours.

I was not in the least fond of my uncle. He had the best room in our apartment and he had the best food. We did without many things so that he could have his education. And when he was ungrateful, which he often was, my mother would say, "But I promised my mother." A deathbed wish had to be carried out at any cost. A healthier response, I feel, would have been rage toward a mother who used her dying moments to exploit her daughter. But thinking of this sort would have been shameful in those times. Mother was sacrosanct.

I, however, was a child, and had not yet been pummeled into acknowledging society's niceties so I often wished my uncle would die (no one told me that murderous childish wishes did not come true). This, too, accentuated my bad seed feelings. However, I decided I would beat my uncle at his game. I told my sister that when I grew up I too was going to be a doctor and I would open my office directly across from my uncle's and steal all his patients. When she asked me how I was going to do that, I replied, with all confidence, that I would serve free frankfurters.

In the end, the effect on me of my uncle's presence in our household (apart from the fact that I developed a negative image of all medical doctors, except for my daughter the cardiologist) was to lead me to think that going to college to become a doctor would make one a pretty important person. It also seemed a fine way to get out of our East Harlem tenement with its bathtub full of gin. That is to say, as a young girl around New York delivering contraband booze, I began thinking of becoming a doctor, i.e. of being a success, as a surefire way to avoid degradation.

Success therefore had nothing to do with inner fulfillment, but rather with an excessive need for outside approval. Success meant becoming above reproach, it meant being out of the reach of those who might destroy me for no reason at all.

On the first leg toward that goal, I threw myself into academic competition as though my very existence depended on victory. Which, of course, given the dynamics of my Family Olympics, ended up being an undertaking filled with a whole lot of misery. Because of my rivalries with my mother and sister all competitive activities were tinged with a sense of imminent danger.

In elementary school, I could still manage to hang in there to win, but never without trauma. Once, in the eighth grade, I competed for a medal for excellence in geography, history, and civics. The medal was to be in the form of a ten-dollar gold coin and it would be presented on graduation day by the then mayor's wife, Mrs. Jimmy Walker. Fearing that I might not win made me almost physically ill; when I did win, I was so hysterical I cried all the way to the stage. I gave the award to my mother, who was in Bellevue Hospital on a ward. My feeling was that if I won it for my mother, and not for myself, it would redeem me for my underlying malevolence, which is how I interpreted my competitive maneuvers. After all, I had destroyed many classmates in my run for that medal.

It was in high school that my pulling back from the brink of success solidified. One pattern that plagued me through those years was to get top marks in all subjects save one, and that subject I'd fail.

Once, I failed my high school math regents and when I had to spend the summer traveling on hot, smelly subways to a classroom far from my home to repeat the course, I felt a sense of jubilation for the penance I was paying. It was a good example of the joy of suffering.

By the time I was ready for college I understood, as did most women of my time, that we did not become doctors like my uncle. At best, we could become doctors' wives. So I enrolled in a school of social work at a southern college.

For a while, my fear of success abated and one semester I managed to get A's in every subject. Delighted, I sent my grades home. In return I received a letter from my father, who rarely wrote to me, saying that he was deeply concerned about my grades. Getting A's, he wrote, meant that I couldn't possibly be having any fun, and he cautioned me that all work and no play would make Martha a dull girl. And being dull in our family, as I mentioned, might lead to abandonment. His message also carried a note of warning that it was okay for me to have a profession—these were the depression years—but being outstanding might make me "too big for my britches." In other words, Dad felt I would abandon him if I became successful. All of this put me in a no-win bind. I had to do well academically to maintain my scholarship status. However, I never got straight A's again.

I became a political activist in my junior year in college. Both my psychology and sociology professors tutored me in political science and I became an apt student. Before long I was engaged in cloak-and-dagger routines such as hiding union organizers in my dormitory room. This may sound bland today, but it was harrowing in the thirties in the South. It also guaranteed that in my senior year I would not get a good field placement in a social work agency. And that meant I would not be employable after graduation. Although this may appear to be a case of self-sabotage, and thus an example of the fear of success, I don't designate it as such. My political activism has always been a source of strength to me and has never failed to bring with it a feeling of internal success.

However, internal success notwithstanding, upon graduation the reality factor of not being able to get a job in my field had to be dealt with. I dealt with it by getting married.

My parents were totally in accord with this decision of mine to marry. And, for a while, so was I. I managed to repress my sense of being useless and I coasted along, filling my time by doing volunteer work for the Spanish Loyalist cause. It was after the birth of my first son that a feeling of restlessness grabbed hold of me again.

It had been a difficult delivery for both of us. My son had a series of convulsions and had to remain in the hospital after I went home. This turn of events precipitated a depression in me that lasted for several weeks. I rallied only when my son was released from the hospital. As soon as my son was out of danger, I again sank into inertia. I was beginning to feel that the role of wife and mother, to the exclusion of all else, was stifling. I felt I was in danger: if I spent all my time washing diapers and cleaning, I would become as desperate as the women of my childhood, women whom I vowed I would never emulate. My political work relieved the monotony of my days, but I needed something more. I wanted intellectual stimulation and an opportunity to utilize my college training.

After much vacillation, needing desperately to gain some perspective on my own identity aside from that of wife and mother, I took a part-time job in a nursery school. The staff consisted of a hotbed of Freudians and it rubbed off, at least at that time, to the extent that I went into analysis five times a week with, as I mentioned, a traditional Freudian. Both of these moves, therapy and a job, were tremendously positive steps.

At the nursery school, I noticed that some of the children in the five- to six-year-old group who were highly intelligent were having difficulty learning to read. They could talk, even hold adult-level conversations, but they stumbled over the easiest texts, whereas some children who were not as well endowed were forging ahead rapidly. It didn't take long before I was itching to go to graduate school. Maybe I could specialize in helping children who had learning problems and help solve this educational mystery.

I had made this decision in a matter of days and was terribly excited, but ten years passed before I actually got to graduate school. By that time, I had two other children for a total of three and a big surburban household and all that it entailed.

When I finally did it, when I finally got myself enrolled in graduate school at the age of thirty-five, I promptly caught pneumonia that kept me in bed for six weeks, enough time to blow the whole first semester.

But I persevered. And, interestingly, after that first setback, I went through the master's degree program relatively free of anxiety. At that time I was so burdened with so many reality problems, I literally felt I had no time to feel privileged. I was paying my dues: I was looking after a husband and three children and a big house; my mother died; my father had a heart attack and came to live with us. I remember taking exams feeling so heavy with trouble that, depleted of energy, I wrote without thinking too deeply. I did well on the exams.

In retrospect, I realize that I did well during my master's program because not all that much was at stake. Those were the bridging years, years that would qualify me for the big battle, the final education hurdle, the doctoral program. It was all right to have succeeded at the preliminary. Nobody was going to punish me for such a relatively minor achievement.

Right on schedule, my fear of success blossomed during my doctoral training. It was then that I almost self-destructed.

I started my sabotage by alienating some of my professors. Fortunately, my adviser picked up on my destructive behavior. He pointed out to me that I used humor to dilute my effectiveness. He enjoyed me, he said, but he showed me that in order to gain attention I was presenting myself as less than a serious person. I was, of course, performing for Daddy but, unlike in childhood, it boomeranged.

Another example of my self-sabotage was the time I had to take a qualifying exam for certification for the doctorate. The evening before the exam I went to a wedding, got home late, got up early, took a Dexamyl for the exam, fell asleep during it, and flunked. Until a professor/psychotherapist informed me that I was intent on failing, I had no idea that I had choreographed the whole thing. He asked me if I had felt elated when I learned I hadn't passed. I looked at him as if he were unbalanced. But then I remembered that after finding out I had failed, I went out and bought myself a very expensive dress. His interpretation was that this was my reward for failing.

What contributed to my fear of success at this time was the enormity of my guilt for having left my children for graduate school. When they complained about my absence I became defensive and said, "When you're grown up you'll be happy to have a mother who is a professional." This brought forth such anger that I was tempted to give up. My husband, who felt I would be impossible to live with if I didn't finish, urged me to see it through.

I managed to get through the course work but the old anxiety and guilt and sense of fraudulence and fear of exposure came to full flower and landed with an iron grip on my attempts to write my doctoral dissertation. It was my last educational battle and true to my fear of success, I almost lost it.

The first roadblock I set up was my quandary regarding which area of research would be the most productive, not for me, but for all mankind. This attitude insures instant paralysis. I thus depleted my energy for a long time, until I realized that my time was running out at the university and I might not be able to make an important contribution to the world of science after all.

I thought my first subject might make a contribution to the controversy regarding the "disadvantaged" child. After I had collected tons of data and had reviewed the literature, my faculty adviser pointed out that I was doing an independent piece of research that, although it might be valuable, was mostly unrelated to the discipline for which I was being trained, that of marriage and family life.

Next I got on with a study that seemed as if it would have limited application in the real world but would get me through the doctorate. However, my design was so complicated that I found myself in a pool of confusion, self-induced of course. It took a faculty member with a long pointer to rescue me. He steered me in a direction that seemed simple but had been so elusive when I was trying to complicate my life in order not to succeed.

Not only did I thwart myself to avoid success, but since I had heard others talk about the incredible tortures of a doctoral dissertation, I had to experience as much pain or perhaps even more to be authentic. When I reviewed the literature from journals, I not only read articles related to my study but I read others that had little or no application. My time in the library consumed me. Soon I had a bibliography that could have been published independently as an anthology of marriage and family life. I was beginning to see that even if I spent a full year in the stacks, all I would get for it was a writing block. So I began to write.

At first I wrote easily, but it was always the first page. At one point I had twenty-four versions of page one. I justified my preoccupation with page one as a means of capturing my reader so brilliantly that the acceptance of the project would be a *fait accompli*. I got to page two when my adviser requested a work progress report. The request sounded to me like a threat. I complied. I wrote almost as many versions of page two as I had of page one, but page three and four became a little, not a whole lot, but a little easier.

I was on the verge of becoming a Ph.D. dropout when a wise psychologist said to me, "Why such a fuss? Nobody's going to read it anyway; it'll just gather dust on some college library shelf, and it'll certainly never be published. If you're meant to do important work, you'll do it after you get out of school."

I stopped obsessing, took a month off from my jobs, and finished my dissertation. While it's admittedly no major contribution to world science, it was a major contribution to my psyche. I had finished something important to me. It was, of course, a matter of not magnifying what I was trying to accomplish.

Minimizing the importance of a goal is an excellent way to reach that goal. A young woman who was scheduled to audition for a symphony orchestra slot and was beside herself with anxiety, told herself that her playing of a flute solo was not going to save anyone's life, and was not going to make the world safe from Fascism. She said to herself, I'm just going to play a little music. So what if I'm the youngest woman ever to audition for the slot? Even if I make a mistake, no one will die, no one will be harmed.

Few of us are ever faced with life-and-death situations in our attempts to reach a goal, yet too many of us act as if we are facing just such situations. As in the case of my doctoral dissertation and in the case of the young flutist's audition, minimizing the importance of the goal that to us seemed so monumental helped us to overcome our fear of success in these instances.

In addition to minimizing a goal, it is always a good idea to slow down the process of success once the goal is at hand. This is especially important for the young. Too much too soon can be disastrous. Success is easier to integrate if you have worked hard for it and maybe even suffered a little for it. Then you can say, without a sense of fraudulence, that you deserve it. You've paid your dues.

A young actor who at age twenty-five won a theater award that brought him dreamed-of Broadway and Hollywood offers, found it a little difficult to handle his overnight success. I recommended that for a while he continue in the TV soap opera that had been his bread-and-butter work before winning the theater award. There was something about getting up at 5 A.M. in Manhattan to go to work in a cold Brooklyn film studio that put into perspective all the fuss people were making over him. I also recommended that instead of moving from his tenement directly to a Park Avenue duplex that he slow down the process of success by taking a less grand apartment. To know that he would never have to work quite as hard as he had before his success was enough success for a while. Other goodies could be integrated gradually.

There exists a marvelous letter George Bernard Shaw wrote to Jascha Heifetz. It reads:

MY DEAR MR. HEIFETZ:

My wife and I were overwhelmed by your concert. If you continue to play with such beauty, you will certainly die young. No one can play with such perfection without provoking the jealousy of the gods. I earnestly implore you to play something badly every night before going to bed.*

What Shaw was advising Heifetz to do, primitive man does almost by instinct—he sacrifices to the gods. If a hunt has been successful, the gods have to be paid off. Primitive society has built-in trade-offs for success. Our civilized trade-offs aren't so automatic.

By trade-off, I don't mean something drastic like exchanging emotional success for work success or vice versa (even though many people do just this). They say, "Who has everything? No one is entitled to have everything." I would answer, "What's everything? A good career and a good emotional life? Is that too much to ask?" I don't think it is.

The sort of trade-off I'm talking about is, for example, the one the young actor made by continuing to act in the soaps for a while. Here's another. . . .

A woman had both areas of her life flourishing. Her career was thriving and she and her new lover were thriving. But something was bothering her: she was upset that she was fifteen pounds overweight. I told her not to lose the weight at the moment, that it might put her in jeopardy. She ignored the advice and lost seventeen pounds through a fast. On the one hand, the suffering of the fast made the weight loss acceptable, but with her new body image she began to find fault with her lover. Only when a minor crisis in her career developed

* As quoted in Rollo May, *The Courage to Create* (New York: W. W. Norton, 1975).

and she gained back ten pounds did her life stabilize. Her lover returned to a position of good standing and her career problem was straightened out. Once again both areas of her life are thriving. The trade-off for the moment is to keep the extra weight. It can be shed in good time, once all of the success has been lived with for a while and integrated.

As we have seen, the fear of success—not getting what we want because we don't feel entitled to it—can manifest itself in any number of ways, both in our work lives and in our love lives. And as we also have seen, the roots of the fear of success lie in our Family Olympics (some of us feel more entitled to success than others because competition patterns in our families were healthier) and in our culture's double messages regarding winning and losing.

To overcome the fear of success, we first have to recognize that we have it, and for this we must get in touch with what and who we genuinely are rather than what and who we perceive ourselves to be. In this quest for self-awareness we may find we don't care for the real us all that much. Our next step is to discover why we have such low self-esteem and that necessitates a trip into our Family Olympics. The goal is to become fonder of ourselves, for as we do so we will feel more entitled to be happy in our work and love lives.

In this self-discovery search we may find that patterns of behavior we once considered merely minor neurotic offshoots not to be taken seriously (e.g., never being able to get anywhere on time) are the very things that have interfered with our quest for success. Once we recognize that these behavior patterns, rather than being harmless eccentricities, are actually sabotaging us, our next step consists of trying to change the patterns.

At this point, for some of us, depending on the severity of our fear of success, therapy or counseling may be needed to root out the underlying dynamics that have led to the self-defeating behavior. For others the many books, articles, case histories, classes, lectures, workshops, and study programs that deal with the theory of the fear of success can, through example, enable us to recognize our own self-defeating behavior and to be on the lookout for things that we do that inevitably lead to disappointment.

It was not until I had revised my estimate of my early childhood that I came to terms with my own fear of success. It was only then that I was able to understand the source of my guilt and my fear of accomplishment. My first reaction was intense rage toward my father, who I felt had set me up. I was equally enraged with my mother for allowing the triangle to flourish at my expense. And I was enraged with them both for pitting me and my sister against each other. With that break-through came the awareness that I no longer had to pay dues; my guilt on the Oedipal score and the sibling score was alleviated. It had taken me years to get to that point.

In polite society, I am what is known as a late bloomer. I don't mind in the least being a late bloomer. How much better than never to have bloomed at all.

Whether our fear of success is ruining our lives or just quietly making us unhappy, a start on the road to overcoming the fear can be undertaken on our own. It is surprising and exhilarating to make discoveries about ourselves in this manner. If we should get stuck along the road, professional help through private thera-pists, clinics, school or job counseling programs, or community mental health centers might be called for. It is fortunate that such help is now generally available.

It is important to point out, however, that in ex-treme cases, some people's success phobia is so monu-mental that no therapeutic intervention currently known to the field of mental health can alleviate the anxiety. These people, who may find it all but impossible' to function in their work lives and their love lives, may need to restructure their lives and settle for lesser goals.

After years of unhealthy sabotage, I can now, without too much trauma, integrate a measure of suc-cess into my life. How do I feel successful?

I'm in the process of leaving my clinic work at Metropolitan Hospital in New York City's East Harlem. Of the psychological hats I have worn—working with children with learning disabilities, seeing private pa-tients, doing clinic work, teaching at the New School, writing about the fear of success—the hat that I consider to have been the most significant is the one I wore while teaching Family Life–Sex Education to groups of schizophrenic patients.

Among them was Jack, a catatonic who began to talk after a silence of many months. For me, that brought a moment of exultation that was private and elevating. Incidentally, once Jack started to talk you couldn't shut him up; others in the class said they liked him better before his breakthrough.

And there was Sandra, a young woman who had been in and out of hospitals most of her life and had been diagnosed as a "no hope" patient. She's now a working painter in SoHo. I go to all of her openings; no one can possibly know what I feel inside.

And there is the young man who called me late at night a few months ago from Cleveland. When he was in my clinic class at the hospital he was addicted to heroin. He called to tell me that he was graduating from college and he was sending me an invitation to the ceremonies. "I met you at a strategic time in my life," he said. "I had almost given up. You helped me to see that I could take another chance at it all. I just wanted you to know that I took it."

I'm not saying that I cured any of these three people of their schizophrenia. But I am saying that they can live outside of a hospital now, and function in our society as it is structured. In treating schizophrenics there are not too many outstanding success stories. But for these three, and some others, I feel an *inner* core of strength that I call success.

Outside recognition is important. We need people to know that we can do something well—but it's only the icing on the cake. More important, in fact crucial, is that we ourselves, deep within, need to know this fact.

Because I'm about to give up teaching the classes in which I met these three patients, and countless others, a colleague and I decided to videotape one of my classes. I almost sabotaged this project by waiting until the very last minute to tape a class; I had had years to record this work but I waited until I almost bowed out. And then, during the taping, I partially sabotaged by making sure I was never on camera. (My colleague reassured me by saying, "With that voice, who else could it be?")

The videotape was a gift to myself; it's a record of the most socially useful thing I've done. I used an innovative approach in dealing with schizophrenics, and watching them grow is my success story. With a sense of *inner* achievement, I have put the videotape into a box and have filed it away in a closet. This is the first time I've spoken of it.

My own overcoming of the fear of success is not ended; it's an ongoing struggle. I still have to be on guard, but now I can recognize when the fear starts to come out from under its rock and, with my understanding of it, I can try to do something about it. Even though I'm a so-called expert on the subject, I'm just like everyone else—I still have insecurities. The many ways in which I tried to sabotage the writing of this book, for example, amazed even me; and during the writing of this particular chapter I had to admit to some lingering anxiety over Telling Family Secrets. Your mother was a *bootlegger*?

It is my hope that these pages have armed you with a basic lay person's understanding of the theory of the fear of success that eventually will enable you to recognize and steer clear of the sort of self-sabotaging behavior in which I and so many others described in this book have indulged. Thus armed, I don't see any reason why you cannot begin to try, as Karen Horney once so simply and beautifully put it, "living up to . . . potentialities and . . . enjoying what life has to offer."*

* Karen Horney, *The Neurotic Personality of Our Time* (New York: W. W. Norton, 1937).